A GARIOCH MISCELLANY

4 NELSON STREET
Garioch's "deeded stane-and-lime property" in Edinburgh's New Town

> . . . unkenn'd uplifted tons of mason-wark piled on the soil,
> wi causey-streets, biggit of granite setts, like blank waas flat on the grund,
> plainstane pavements of Thurso slabs laid owre the stane-aircht cellars,
> the area fifteen feet doun, wi weill-jyned flagstanes, Regency wark.
>
> (from "Brither Worm")

A GARIOCH MISCELLANY

SELECTED AND EDITED

BY

ROBIN FULTON

LINES REVIEW EDITIONS

MACDONALD PUBLISHERS
EDINBURGH

ISBN 0 86334 057 1

Published in 1986 by
Macdonald Publishers
Loanhead, Midlothian EH20 9SY

*The publisher acknowledges the financial
assistance of the Scottish Arts Council
in the publication of this volume.*

Printed in Scotland by
Macdonald Printers (Edinburgh) Limited
Edgefield Road, Loanhead, Midlothian EH20 9SY

Contents

The Good Lord excelled Himself
in His creation of
Robert Garioch

Preface

This short miscellany is intended to complement the recently published collected edition of Robert Garioch's poems and it aims to give a picture of Garioch as man-of-letters which those who knew him will recognise and cherish and which ought to widen the interest of those who knew him only through his poetry.

As a prose-writer Garioch's *forte* was his ability to comment on the scene around him: the scene always included people, it often included books, pictures and music, and the commentary would illustrate, again and again, how he could bring his reading of literature and history to bear upon the specific instances of human generosity or folly which caught his attention. As a prose-writer he was not "inventive" — by which I mean that writing fiction did not seem to interest him much. (The early notebooks contain some attempts at short-story writing but he did not seem happy with them.) He was the kind of writer to whom the "real" world around him was in itself so intriguing, immediate, comic or horrifying that fiction was unnecessary. The sterling qualities of *Two Men and a Blanket* may well make us wish that he had written more prose: admittedly, the account of his P.O.W. experiences was "the story of a lifetime" and could hardly have been repeated, but I am sure that if he had been given the right kind of encouragement he could well have produced a body of prose whose interest would have fallen not far short of that of his poetry.

As it is, the bulk of his prose (apart from the war-time autobiography) is to be found in his letters. I have tried to give here a selection which I hope will indicate the nature and range of his letter-writing. Fortunately for us, as onlookers or eavesdroppers, he tended to use pen and paper rather than the telephone, and while much of his correspondence concerned literary business he seldom confined himself merely to the matter in hand: observations, recollections, speculations and fancies would spill over into addenda and postscripts, often crowding into the margins and corners of fragile scraps of paper. The only instance where I have not been selective is in the case of his correspondence with Antonia Stott: I have given this almost complete because it shows in detail how he worked on the Belli translations.

7

Of the letters from which I have chosen extracts, those up to and including June 1958 were written from 90 Constance Crescent, Hayes, Bromley, Kent. The rest were written from 4 Nelson Street, Edinburgh. Most of them open fairly formally (Dear Mrs Stott, Dear Caird) even when the recipient is well-known; the letters to J. K. Annand and to Sydney Tremayne are the only ones I have seen which consistently open with a christian name. The customary ending is "Yours sincerely," followed by any one of the following eight variations: Robert G. Sutherland, Sutherland, Robert Garioch, Robert G., Robert G. S., Robert Garioch Sutherland, Robert Garioch (Sutherland), or Robert Garioch S. The recipient of each letter is of course indicated, but those marked "To a Friend" were sent to a recipient who wishes to remain anonymous.

Selecting from Garioch's reviews was less difficult. He reviewed only intermittently, so there was less to choose from. I have, besides, not included any of his "round-up" reviews (such as his reviews of novels for *The Listener* from June 1970 to January 1971): I suspect he was given that type of review because he could be relied on to do a competent job promptly. I have selected, rather, from those reviews where he was able to comment on only one book or author at a time.

Whether he would have wanted to review books regularly I do not know, but I think it is a pity that his talents in this direction were not employed more often and in periodicals with a wide circulation. His reviewing practices and manners not only contain a useful lesson or two for many busier reviewers but also illustrate basic aspects of his attitude both to the business of writing and to his fellow writers. Some of these aspects can be suggested on the basis of a few quotations.

First, a mere passing remark, while reviewing *Scottish Poetry Eight* in *Lines Review* No. 57: "reporting, which is my immediate job." It may seem too obvious to mention that a reviewer's primary function is to *report*, if it were not for the fact that many reviewers forget it. On the one hand we have a new book, on the other, a potential reader: the latter has not seen the former and needs information of quite an elementary kind. Description is an inescapable part of a reviewer's task: he is not being asked to abandon his critical function but if he offers instant judgment without description he is doing both the writer and the potential reader an unmannerly disservice. Garioch never forgot that basic starting-point. And, it should be added, he did not let elegant and craftsmanlike design and printing-work pass unpraised.

Second, another passing remark, this time from his review of Andrew Young's *Collected Poems* in *Lines Review* No. 50: "poetry quietly asserts itself, and not a single lecturer in English Literature, one confidently believes, can do anything about it." Garioch's genuine respect for scholarship is not in question here: what this remark suggests to me is the manner in which his considerable experience of non-literary life influenced his approach to writing, and this in several ways. He was always aware of the practicalities of writing, publishing and reading; he never forgot how for most writers literature feeds from life and in turn feeds back into life, and for most readers books have to find their place among many, often pressing, non-bookish activities. This saved him from the kind of tiredness that often seems to overcome professional literary people, to whom most things are *déjà vu* and whose appetite can be tickled only by what is "new." It helped him too to retain a capacity for surprise and curiosity, an ability to find interest and pleasure in things which perhaps a more narrowly literary critic would pass over. He touches on this in his comments on Michael Hamburger in *Lines Review* No. 49 and his reference to Edwin Muir, "who lived quietly, spending much of his time in practical jobs," while keeping a certain "core of commitment," could be applied to himself.

The third sample is longer and comes from his review in *Lines Review* No. 66 of a long poem by Walter Perrie: "If 'She,' the most powerful being in this poem, is the 'Life Force,' that is something I have viewed with suspicion for many years, and I have long had my doubts about that passage from Canto LXXXI that is here given out as the poem's text. Also, in respect of the form of a long poem, I cannot regard Pound as a useful influence. Mr Perrie has put forth impressive strength in writing this difficult poem, but the cumulative method, though never discursive, does leave work to the reader that would have been better done by the author; I think the poem is a success, but it does more harm than good, I think, to make that success so far from obvious."

I have singled out this passage as one of the most extreme examples I could find of Garioch's way of expressing doubts about a work under review. Advocates of hard-hitting journalism may simply complain that Garioch pulled his punches: I have always felt that hard-hitting reviews tell us more about the pent-up aggressions and envies of the reviewer than they tell us about the book in question and I suspect Garioch would have agreed. The point about the quoted remarks is that while quite clearly expressing doubts Garioch did not discourage the potential reader. As one writer discussing the work of another he never lost sight of the simple fact that writing costs effort, and when he saw some success in the enterprise he said so. He knew that a book means something to its author too.

A fourth aspect I would like to mention needs no specific example here: his craftsmanlike approach to verse-making. His reviews of poetry show his practical interest in metre and rhyme, and he was not afraid of dictionaries. After all, scansion and etymology greatly concern the writer: they should equally concern the reviewer.

Acknowledgements are due to many: to the magazines in which the reprinted reviews first appeared; to the recipients of letters who sent me copies for the purposes of this book; and then to the staffs of The National Library of Scotland, The University of Newcastle Library, The University of Reading Library, and The John Rylands University Library of Manchester. But I would especially like to express my thanks to those who wrote to me, not only suggesting possible sources of letters but also recounting reminiscences of Garioch—or simply recording their admiration for him. The remark quoted at the very beginning of this book (from a letter from Mrs Mary MacDonald) sums up what many of his life-long friends felt.

ROBIN FULTON

Growing Up ROBERT GARIOCH

The first thing I remember about growing up is dismay—when I realised that I had *stopped* growing. I'd been accustomed to growing, all those years, and took it for granted, supposing this would go on until I was about as tall as my father. Ah well, I grew a little taller than my mother, then I had to admit that I had stopped, at just about five feet five, if I stretched my neck. Only people who are still growing up will understand how upset I was. I can't even understand it myself, now. Five feet five, I've since discovered, is the very best height. Not too short, not too tall. But I know now that when you are growing up you are sure to be a bit worried about what sort of deal you are being handed out by fate. And only people who have grown up will understand that we're all rather pleased with ourselves, once we've found out what Nature intended to make of us. That's one comfort, anyhow.

Another awkward thing is that Nature decides when we are grown up, though we still can't think of ourselves as men. A Jewish boy becomes a man, officially, on his thirteenth birthday, so there's no doubt about it, and that must be a big help in some ways, though Jewish boys I used to know would tell me that it didn't seem to make much difference, after all. They still had to go to school. The leaving age was fourteen in those days.

You'll notice I'm only talking about boys and men, though the girls can listen if they want to. I knew almost nothing about girls in those days. I had no sisters, and the few girl-cousins of about my own age, I treated with suspicion, and very great caution, I don't know why. I met girls mostly at parties and got the idea that if you touched them they had pins sticking out everywhere, and strings of beads that broke and rolled over the floor. They were better left alone, I thought. And I was right, for once. There's no hurry, after all.

I mentioned the school leaving age, fourteen in my day. I took no notice of that. I was more concerned with The Leavings. That wasn't something you gave to the cat, but the Higher Leaving Certificate. I swotted very hard for that, and collected a good average set of passes. We all swotted, willingly enough, I think, or nearly all of us. Times were hard, and we knew it. I was five when the First World War started, and I grew up in a country suffering from terrible unemployment and poverty. I was lucky to be still at school, at my father's expense. He left school at twelve to earn some money, because his mother was left a widow, and he wanted to give me a better chance of education than he had himself.

I was growing up in a maindoor house in Bellevue Road, Edinburgh, and considered myself lucky because we were so well-off, and we had electric light, and I had a second-hand bike with an oil-lamp, and we were altogether rather posh. Don't scoff. There were boys in my class at school who could beat me at French and Maths, though not at English, who never had enough to eat.

But what about this business of growing up? I can't remember all that much. It was terribly important at the time, and full of promise, and frightening. But, if I had only known, I didn't need to worry. I worried about Maths, of course, and all that sort of thing, and quite right, too. You've got to be serious about work. But you needn't worry about yourself, all that much. I thought I was terribly clumsy-looking and worried very much about that. Well, maybe I was, maybe I wasn't. But that was all right. It didn't matter if I wasn't like a fellow called Arnot, in the Fifth Year, who was strong and graceful, and could putt the shot, and was good-looking, and became a famous ballet-dancer. We all thought he was wonderful, and so he was. But so were we all, each in his own way. And so are you.

But don't get stuck-up about it.

— Undated MS in The National Library of Scotland

A Recollection

SORLEY MACLEAN

The following is Sorley Maclean's contribution to the Scotsoun cassette *In Mind o a Makar, Robert Garioch 1909-1981* (SSC 061) and is reproduced here with the kind permission of Scotsoun.

When I came to Edinburgh University in October 1929 Robert Garioch Sutherland was beginning his fourth year. I got to know him very soon through his friend in the same year, Jack Stewart from Laggan in Badenoch, one of the very finest men I have ever known. I'd attached myself to Edinburgh University shinty team, in which Jack's brother Ellis, then in his second year, was a most brilliant player. Robert was already one of the best known of the poets appearing in *The Student*. He did not, probably because of his Scots, have the prestige of J. D. K. Rafferty, who seemed to many of us as good as the Pound of *Hugh Selwyn Mauberley* at Pound's own game. But I have a secret pride that even then I rated Garioch above the brilliant Rafferty and above many others of his prestige in Scotland and England. I did not know Garioch well during my university days. It was only a case of meetings in the Old Quad, mostly in the company of Jack Stewart, during the session 1929-1930, and then sometimes in the session 1930-1931, when Garioch and Stewart were at Moray House.

After 1931 I hardly ever saw Garioch but during my years of teaching in Portree School from 1934 to 1937 I heard a great deal about him from Jack Stewart. Stewart had a quite marvellous insight into all sorts of people, a breadth and sympathetic generosity of insight which made him, *inter alia*, a teacher of genius. Garioch was one of his great topics of conversation and obviously a great favourite of his, in spite of Garioch's apparent political detachment, which was so different from Stewart's own passionate commitment.

When I came back to Edinburgh early in 1939 I renewed my acquaintance with Garioch but not very soon in 1939. It was not till the autumn of that year that I began to frequent any meetings of writers. When I got to know him really well, in the first months of 1940, I was too much obsessed with a ridiculous dilemma of my own to appreciate him to the full and even to appreciate his great

13

and reticent generosity to myself. He was then staying with his father in Bellevue. They were a wonderful pair with an unusual community of interests, artists, craftsmen and musicians with an unobtrusive mutual affection and loyalty, humorous, unworldly and unpretentious. Garioch's mature poetry and prose is an authentic reflection of a rare, fine and honest human being.

A Personal Memoir DEREK BOWMAN

When I think of Robert Garioch (as I knew him) I see him in that eternal thick grey polo-neck pullover of his, which, he once said, saved him the trouble of laundering shirts. I see his round face, the lively grey hair about his bald pate, his honest eyes. He tended to laugh more than smile — frequently and loudly, explosively even, when the ridiculousness of some piece of human pretension or folly hit him. His laughter, however, was never malicious; he had too much self-knowledge, self-irony for that.

I first got to know him from a distance in the late 1960s through sending off poems to *Scottish International*, of which he was one of the editors. Later I heard him vigorously reading his own work at "Poetry 71," the jamboree organised at the then prosperous Edinburgh University by John Schofield, and also at readings held in the old Chaplaincy Centre at the corner of Forrest Road, and again later at meetings of the literary and folksong club, "The Heretics," in The New Town Hotel in Darnaway Street down in that antique-festooned basement, the lines of his poems punctuated by the rattle of the cash-register at the bar (a feature calculated to appeal to his alert imagination).

One evening in the 1970s I happened to be with him in the lounge of the University Staff Club, probably after a reading, along with a group of poets and their followers. The party decided to go down to the basement bar (the "Id" of the Staff Club): no doubt they'd be making a night of it. Sitting down quietly at a table in the lounge, Robert said to me he didn't favour that at all, himself: they'd only be downing pints wholesale, and although he liked a drink as much as the next man, he was not for over-doing it, at least not on this occasion. I noticed that for all his rumbustiousness, his joviality — you should have heard him read his Caledonian Antisyzygy poem! — there was a fastidious side to him, that choiceness which distinguishes his literary work. Whilst fully appreciating what life has to offer, he was his own man; in a world in which "nae thing's pruven, naethin pruvable," he would draw aside when he felt like it, coolly assess the situation, decide for himself.

I got to know him better when he was Writer in Residence at Edinburgh University (1971-1973), where I work. He took the post

15

seriously, putting in the hours conscientiously. Whenever I wanted to discuss poems of mine that I had submitted to him for criticism, he was always to be found in his room in the David Hume Tower, sitting at the table by the window overlooking George Square. His notebook would be lying open before him, full of jottings, different versions of translations, suggestions for rhymes: to aid him he possessed a rhyming dictionary among his other generally well-worn old-fashioned reference books. He not only criticised my own writing constructively, but I noticed he went out of his way to help younger poets to place their work.

Later in the 1970s I came to know Robert personally. He came round to my house on a couple of occasions for the evening, and my family and I might call on him and his wife Peggie at their flat in Nelson Street on a Sunday afternoon (that difficult Scottish time). After his wife died I used to call round once every two or three weeks, particularly during the autumn and winter months, when I'd take a couple of cans of Export or Skol, or perhaps some German schnapps.

After pulling the huge brass handle of the bell to the right of his door, marked "IV," I'd hear his footsteps along the passage, then the great door would creak open to the slight rattle of a chain; he'd greet me warmly and we'd go downstairs — I always admired the unique, curved art-nouveau door at the bottom—then through to Robert's living-room at the back, which was heated by a coal fire. Along one wall hung a row of beautiful water-colours by his old friend Sydney Goodsir Smith. The room would usually be full of books and papers, magazines and letters, on tables and chairs, and overflowing into the kitchen. Behind a full bookcase to the right, topped with a couple of cardboard boxes containing those hundreds and hundreds of Guiseppe Belli sonnets in several paperback volumes, there was situated Robert's own special cubby-hole in a recess — a real Cave of Making. He'd invariably ask me which seat I preferred, and I would sit to the left of the fireplace, with my back to the window, he to the right. After he'd brought two freshly-rinsed pint glasses from the kitchen we'd pull up our armchairs to the fire. I'd light my pipe and we'd talk for hours, with him occasionally stoking up the fire, dispassionately watched by the small embossed profile of David Hume set in a frame on the wall to the right.

I loved to hear about Robert's army days and school-teaching experience down in London. I too had been through the mill, and knew exactly what he was talking about. I was glad his findings agreed with mine. I also found him very understanding when I told him of some of the current odd, sometimes hurtful goings-on in the academic world. Though he had a good opinion of Grierson, and of some of his own teachers at the Royal High School, he was never taken in by fussy headmasters, pompous pundits, astute literary operators and suchlike privileged nuisances, however powerful: empty authority, red tape (i.e. bull-shit) was anathema to both of us.

He was under no illusions regarding the aggressive demands of teenage lads either and the cruelty they can display towards any weakness — or what they regard as such — on the part of schoolteachers. He himself had been disappointed, I believe, by the brutishness of such teenagers in his charge, and had been on one occasion so provoked that he was tempted to use corporal punishment. There and then he decided it was time for him to leave the profession. I also remember Robert observing that schoolchildren's assessments of their teachers could be utterly mistaken. Similarly he made no bones about the laziness and greed of all too many British factory workers and their short-sighted Trades Unions in the 1960s and 1970s. He was not taken in by slack disgruntled talk about "changing the system," nor was he at all impressed by the cavortings of the lavish sixties and early seventies — flower-power, the drug culture, hippydom, the pop cult. . . . He was outraged, as indeed I was, at the massive wrongness of the decisions of many so-called "town-planners" all over Britain, especially in his beloved Edinburgh, at that time. He agreed that the University had done infinite harm by insensitively destroying whole organic communities in the Southside. He was particularly hurt, since he always had a strong sense of the quality of ordinary people's lives, the character of localities, the vital health of neighbourhood communities, the shops, trades, pubs, the life about the streets, talk, the local vernacular. Doesn't much of his poetry indeed spring from this love? I recall the affection with which he always spoke of Leith, of his father and his work as a painter and decorator. Although Robert owned a motor-bike, which he typically kept on into its old age, somehow I always think of him as a pedestrian, grimacing "vroom vroom" at passing cars. He needed to take his time, take things in.

Loyal to Scotland, he was never narrowly nationalistic, nor unthinkingly anti-English, indeed he found some of the extremist manifestations of Scottish nationalism disturbing, and wrote a letter to that effect to the magazine *Calgacus*. His tolerance can be seen in the way he included English-born poets like myself, living in Scotland, in his anthology *Made in Scotland* (1974). He was truly cosmopolitan, loving literature wherever it grew and thrived.

Robert had a lively sense of literary tradition, as can be seen in his work on George Buchanan (whose picture hung in his living room), Sir David Lindsay and especially Robert Fergusson, with whom he felt a close affinity. Like many poets, he was an avid translator, casting his net widely to include an unusually wide catch. As a reader he was particularly fond of Raymond Queneau's humorous novel *Zazie dans le Métro*, perhaps in part because of the author's use, like Belli, of the demotic style. Amongst English authors he repeatedly referred to Shakespeare, Wordsworth and Keats, and would constantly check any quotations from them. Though he possessed a TV, he was selective in his viewing. He was, however, a keen listener to the radio, especially Radio 3 literary programmes; latterly he much appreciated the readings from Langland's *Piers Plowman*. I remember Robert ringing me up specially to draw my attention to a programme of reminiscences of a nineteenth-century printer. Needless to say he was not impressed by such offerings as "The Tartan Terror Show."

He was always interested to hear what I had to say about German literature, especially my favourite writers, Goethe, Mörike and Fontane. Hegel he found too hard. Of the modern Scottish novelists I remember him speaking appreciatively of Janet Caird and Elspeth Davie; among contemporary poets he praised Sydney Tremayne, Liz Lochhead, Margaret Reynolds and Val Warner. He had, I believe, reviewed novels for *The Listener* for a spell and admired Anthony Burgess's *Abba Abba*; perhaps its subject, the relationship of Belli and Keats and their approach to poetry and language, predisposed him in its favour. Of reviewers I remember him praising Allan Massie and Matthew Moulton.

I believe I detected the influence of David Hume on Robert. I noticed how in conversation he would frequently adopt a benevolently sceptical note on subjects of philosophical nicety or ecclesiastical solemnity, but there was no doubting Robert's democracy, his love of freedom, his respect for human dignity and his sympathy with ordinary people. He spoke highly of George Davie's *The Democratic Intellect* and lent me his own copy, inscribed by the author. Indeed Robert was himself the soul of common sense.

He had a great admiration for James Joyce, knew his work well, and when I visited Dublin in the summer of 1980 he listened with interest to all I had to tell him of the city, especially of such places as Sandy Cove and the Martello Tower. He was particularly fond of *Ulysses*, could gleefully quote whole chunks of it—he had a remarkable memory in this respect—and treasured his own extremely battered early edition of the book. He was very grateful when I lent him my copy of Kevin Sullivan's *Joyce among the Jesuits*, which I'd picked up for £2.25 in an Edinburgh second-hand bookshop. Now I come to think about it, he and Joyce had quite a lot in common, both being confirmed city-lovers with a strong sense of physical reality and common speech. Like Joyce he was fascinated by etymology. I remember how Robert studied intently my collection of old postcards of Liverpool, my home-town. Such cities as Dublin and Liverpool and Edinburgh stood as excellent topographies of life. I recall too the delight with which he would recount his jaunts to poetry-readings in towns: the one to Newcastle-upon-Tyne he described with particular relish.

Talking to Robert was always a tonic. I'd bring him something I'd written, or he'd read out to me his latest contribution as resident bard for Radio Forth, a post he efficiently filled for a number of months with his customary self-deprecating irony; or perhaps it would be one of his latest Belli translations. I found him a great encouragement—what a precious commodity enthusiasm is!—even an inspiration, as doubtless many writers in Scotland have also found in their time. He had a quick sympathy for what one was trying to do in a piece of work; he entered warm-heartedly into one's feelings and thoughts, and he inspired confidence. I can still hear him say "That's *very* good!"

I noticed this generosity repeatedly displayed in his many reviews of new poetry in *Scottish International*, *Lines Review*, or *Akros*, reviews which were refreshingly positive, clear and cogent, and expressed in a simple, lively, *human* style. One felt he knew how much the book meant to its author, as well as judging what value it might have to its potential readers. The tone of his criticism was poles apart from the disdainful note adopted, say, in *The Times*

Literary Supplement. Nor was he taken in by the over-complicatedness of academics who contrive to make literature seem harder than it really is, perhaps to show what clever interpreters they can be. For Robert a good poem had the same essential qualities as a good table: they were both products of craftsman-ship, hence the craftsmen themselves were generally the best people from whom to learn the particular art. Soundness was what counted. He hated mystification in any shape or form.

Being a poet he was of course rooted in the natural world: "Brither Worm," to my mind one of his best poems, exemplifies this. I remember him telling me how he and Peg had once looked after a pigeon for a time that had happened to stray into their flat. (Didn't he term it the "diddie-bird"?) When he was interviewed for a television programme, one of the crew took several photographs of the bird and later presented Robert with enlargements. I forget what happened to the actual bird but I have one of these photographs, which he gave me.

Occasionally he would take in a film in "The Filmhouse" along Lothian Road, an older one, one that he was pretty sure to appreciate, such as *Sur les Toits de Paris* or *La Règle du Jeu*, or some early American comedy. He spoke little of modern films, though he did enjoy the recent Royal Shakespeare Company production of Shakespeare's plays on television. Of the other arts, though there was a piano in his front room upstairs, he spoke little of music and musicians to me, but then he always knew much more than he said. He did have a sharp eye for architecture. I recall his warm praise of The Edinburgh Museum of Antiquities, which I ventured to criticise — this was on the way to his cobbler's — but we both shared admiration for the great round red-painted tower on the opposite corner. Now, I always associate that part of town with him. He loathed the High Street being dubbed The Royal Mile: he hadn't much time for royalty and aristocracy and suchlike high-class exploiters, the airs and graces they affect and the servility they encourage. Robert fully shared Fergusson's rejection of the Scottish establishment's adulation of Dr Johnson. Bigwigs left him cold. His own heroes tended to be of the school of the canny good solder Schweik, hence his sympathy for Ulrich Bräker.

Any letter to Robert received a prompt reply: I noticed too that he liked to display picture-postcards sent to him around his flat, together with particularly treasured objects, like the drawing of his wife and the fine paintings of Edinburgh houses that she did. And indeed any letter from him was a highly characteristic Garioch exercise, the text being full of asides, quips, marginal comments, as he good-naturedly, shrewdly, teased out *his* truth. The envelope in its turn would be covered with bold crossings-out, new name and address substituted, strips of brown paper stuck on here and there like sticking-plaster — he economised on stationery. He was aware of the value of things — he had to be, since he was not particularly well-off, having retired early, nor, as British man of letters, did he receive a just reward for his labours.

He was a great man who never made a fuss. He never received the full measure of recognition to which he was due in his lifetime, but then he'd been long aware that, the world being what it is, people whose first concern it is to tell the truth — even with grace — are bound to offend at times, and not get on. Whatever the case, in his day-to-day living, as in his writings, he remained invariably perceptive and kindly, a rare and irresistible combination. I, for one, am sure that his "twa-three chuckie-stanes," as he called them with characteristic modesty, even humility, will stay put on the Scottish cairn.

Two Comments EDWIN MORGAN

Of the following two comments, the first is the introduction to the Scotsoun cassette *Robert Garioch: Poems selected by Edwin Morgan* (SSC 045), and the second is from the Scotsoun cassette *In Mind o a Makar, Robert Garioch 1909-1981* (SSC 061). Both of these are reproduced here with the kind permission of Scotsoun.

In a letter to Edwin Morgan (14 July 1978) after the first of these cassettes appeared, Garioch wrote: "Thank you for reading my Muir poem so well..., long and difficult, though it does not sound so. I like the sense of urgency and importance this recording gives. Also there is a sense that it is a shortish and hurried poem, with a lot to say and not much time, which I think is a good way to read a long and difficult poem."

I

Robert Garioch (or "Geerie") is the pen-name of Robert Sutherland, born in Edinburgh in 1909, and one of the best-known of those contemporary Scottish poets who write in Scots. Like his eighteenth-century predecessor, Robert Fergusson, whom he likes and admires, Garioch has been thought of as particularly a poet of Edinburgh, and it's true that a good deal of his best work is concerned with that city. Sometimes he writes with great gusto and enjoyment, mainly to entertain, as in "Embro to the Ploy" with its shower of sly digs at the Edinburgh Festival, from naked happenings at the McEwan Hall to the American tourist trade in tartan. This poem, using a variant of the old Scottish bob-wheel stanza, deliberately looks back at the tradition of similar poems of communal merrymaking and high-jinks in Scotland.

In his remarkable series of "Edinburgh Sonnets" Garioch shows his virtuosity within the most difficult of the sonnet forms. But the virtuosity is used to produce stinging rhymes, pointed suspensions of meaning over line-endings, and nice juxtapositions of Scots and English vocabulary. He gives the sonnets quite a range of subject and tone, from the sardonic social comment of "I'm Neutral" and "Did Ye See Me?" through the weird, almost surreal conversation of "Heard in the Cougate" to the straight dignified moving tribute of "At Robert Fergusson's Grave."

As a one-time schoolmaster, Garioch is aware of the attractions of story, fable, and legend. His "Percipient Swan," speaking in the first person, transforms some of the conventions of animal fable into a direct assault on all clippers of wings, so that the idea of an elegantly sad swan-song is stood on its head and becomes a shamanistic rhyming-to-death sung against the oppressors of the free spirit:

> For my sang sall foretell
> no my ain destruction;
> I sall rhyme the end
> of your hale stupid faction.

A similar cautionary tale, "The Canny Hen," takes a hit at battery egg-production and its wider implications, and is composed as a more traditional fable. These two poems use the wing-clipped swan and the mechanised hen as figures that can help to spell out the dangers of authority and control:

> Aa things are sinfu, ye'll agree,
> that dinna suit the pouers that be.
> Whan men or hens begin to think,
> they're unco near perdition's brink.

In a couple of poems that turn to legend for their material, the legends of Faust and Sisyphus, Garioch develops this favourite theme of the limitations of freedom in two different and interesting ways. Sisyphus in the poem of that name is the worker trapped in the toils of the cash-nexus, trundling his burden of labour up to the summit of the next pay-packet, only to have it bounce downhill ready for the next stint. In this poem the imitated classical metre provides a brilliant rhythmical pattern for the movements of the boulder. The other poem, "Doktor Faust in Rose Street," makes the nice point that that great would-be sceptic, Faust, when he appears with his "hippy gear" and "kill-joy luik" in an Edinburgh students' pub, is more shocked and horrified by the students than they are by him, and he has to signal to his master, Satan, to get him out of that hellish environment. And so he's bound to *his* boss in an even deeper contract.

Both of these poems are entertaining, largely comic pieces which have become well-known at poetry-readings; their movement and their word-play are clearly directed towards the speaking voice. But Garioch has also written more meditational, philosophical poems presented without his usual ironies and reversals, and of these "The

Muir" is the most interesting. This is a longer poem which lacks the immediate vivacity of the more comic pieces and demands some concentration of attention but which has real rewards for the patient listener or reader. It's a bold attempt at a scientific poem in Scots. The poet tries to penetrate below the surface life of a Scottish moor on a bright summer day, wrestling with the mystery of its atomic and subatomic life, where the everyday laws we know and use seem to be suspended in the paradoxical, evasive world of the elementary particles. What is real, what is solid, is anything solid left? A striking effect is obtained by bringing in the figure of Robert Fergusson and asking whether Fergusson's fear of Hell when he was mad and in chains is any less real than our own fears of losing the intelligibility of the world we live in. This poem is a valuable extension of the use of Scots into a difficult area.

Among the most notable poems in his later volumes are two which show his characteristic mingling of imagination and observation. "Brither Worm," with its central image of the soft but persistent worm poking through the hard flagstones of a city street, reminds us of Garioch's awareness of the endless tension between the worlds of nature and man. The other poem, "Perfect," develops the same idea through the contrast between a skilled carpenter's craftsmanship and pressing a button so that

> Out comes, say, Honduras mahagony, shade nine...
> ...it's perfect,
> perfect every time.
> And I dinnae like it.

This is not just nostalgia, whether for a world of unpaved roads or of handmade furniture. Garioch is very much a poet of today, even when he criticises it. His poetry is a fine achievement of well-turned, pithy, entertaining verse, not without its more sombre and moving touches when required.

II

I remember Robert Garioch, as I think most people do, with a lot of affection. I always looked forward to meeting him. We were often on the same platform at poetry-readings, and it was quite a study to see how well he understood the poet-audience situation — the fact that somehow, although it's partly a case of people being there to be entertained, it is also a kind of self-revelation — it's both performance and truth. He enjoyed playing the role of the performer, even of the clown, the naïve unworldly bumbling man who can't find the right book or the right poem — though in fact he usually had a careful, numbered list of poems he was going to read! And once he had won the audience over, through humour and sympathy, he equally enjoyed surprising them with straight or serious or sad poems, and he knew that in the end he could present a true overall picture of a more complex character than people had expected.

I always felt the general truth of this: that there was a good deal more to Garioch than met the eye. At the time when we were both involved, with Bob Tait, in editing the magazine *Scottish International*, the two Roberts used to come through from Edinburgh to my place in Glasgow for editorial meetings. Time and again I noticed how unexpected, and sharp, his comments were, even though he liked to project the image — and, after all, it wasn't *entirely* an untrue image — of a conservative and distracted person unaccountably brought into the cut-and-thrust of contemporary ideas. Actually he blossomed out and felt happy in that so-called modish decade of the Sixties, and wrote very productively at that time and into the Seventies. I think he did regret that some of his more obviously serious poems, like the long poem "The Muir," struck a slow response from readers and critics, and in this he may have felt he had overplayed the role of pawky commentator and satirist, as perhaps he had. I think he wanted to make two points: first, that you can be serious in comedy, in entertaining, ironic, sometimes hilarious poems, and second, that the comic writer mustn't be forbidden to write in a different way when he's trying to build up a lengthy and ambitious poem on a serious theme. It's not really the old idea of the clown longing to play Hamlet; it's rather something about Hamlet himself, who loved clowning but had other, darker, voices.

Garioch was a man who loved the exact word, whether in Scots or in English, and in many of his letters to me I was always struck by his emphasis on detail, on the craft of writing, on his delighted discovery of some new word which he could use in one of his translations. Even in his letters he often had a nice turn of phrase. I remember when he was sent Anthony Burgess's book *Abba Abba*, which contains Burgess's translations from Giuseppe Belli, for review, and expressed his surprise by saying, "Am I becoming the Red Adair of the Belli industry?" I noticed one thing about his deep interest in the craftsman's side of poetry (as I'm sure other people did too), and that was that at poetry-readings he would attempt to bring out the form of the verse (in metre or rhyme or whatever) by a curiously studied delivery which one had to get used to, especially as it was going rather against the tide of "expressive" readings. In this he always kept something of the classicist, and that was another part of the picture. I have no doubt about his achievement, but I think it will be some time before the whole man comes into full focus.

Letters — I

[To Ian Fletcher]   (? 1947)

Thank you very much for the notes on Garioch, which Sutherland enjoyed reading....

The Garioch essay pleases me very much and I have none but pleased comments to make, except that it is not true that he is so indifferent about what he does with his poems. The reverse is true, in fact. Never mind.

Note: In the file of letters to IF there is a photocopy of a printed version of "The Bog" (the earlier six-stanza version) and in close writing curling round the entire poem are the following remarks, which presumably date from a time close to that of the above letter:

Sutherland very much interested, or would be if he ever knew what was going on in the literary world. Just remembered an interesting bit of encouragement he got was from the *Scots Observer*, a paper which it would be worth someone's while to study. It died about 1933 or so. Published by *The Hamilton Advertiser*. Morrison, the editor at the time, about 1932, was about the first to take any notice of Garioch—gave him a weekly half-page of Edinburgh notes to write, "The best weekly feature in Scottish journalism," and published his poems, including the "Masque of Edinburgh," which in its day was a blast against the prevailing Edinburgh literati. Don't think you have read it in full. Must show you it some day. It is a kind of unfinished pageant I always mean to finish some day. Morrison was a good man, probably still is. Mention him and Garioch's gratitude, and we'll send a copy of your article to him....

[To Hamish Henderson]   Easter Sunday (?1948)

This letter heading, I hope, is the beginning of the revival of the Chalmers Press; with some trouble I think I could get this machine to work better. I admit I'd like someone to print this poem who would pey me for it, but that no doubt is unlikely. I sent it to the *Weakly Scotsman* and it immediately bounced back with a wee prentit slip intillt. Bit that's jist ti be expeckit, it wudnae dae ti blaw the gaff on onything avaw. It seems moreanmare that we have to earn our leeving somehow and thereby keep some poetry going for fun, at the lowest notion: eddificatioun we may forget meantime.

With this end in view I went on Thursday to Twickenham and got some equipment to set going the wee printing press I got via Sydney Smith, and hope sometime to get out anither wee book. It seems this sort of thing is the most feasible nowadays.

The drawback, of course, is the time involved in typesetting and all that, when spare time is from 6 to about 11 on a week-night, but by doing a wee bit at a time it might get done. If it is possible to bind single leaves of 4to I should like to do it that way, numbering the pages as I go, and issuing this book when I felt like it, adding bits on the end from time to time, with a wee change added to the fly-leaf. It seems a very feasible idea, though hard on the patience and consequently very expensive in the matter of beer. But there again, that might be attended to on the same principle by brewing my own.

[To Ian Fletcher] (?1954)

I got a copy of *Chanticlere* this week and felt very grateful to you.... The point is that no appreciation of Garioch's poems has ever been written before, and if I had stayed in Scotland it would not have been written yet, certainly not by anyone there. What I am grateful for is that you took the trouble to do it, and found somebody to print it.

I've been reading Isaac's book *Background to Modern Poetry*. According to him there is only one kind of modern poetry, and it's certainly not my kind. All the same, it makes me think how good it must be to know what to do and to learn how to do it. Can you tell me, if one is not an Imagist or a Symbolist, or whatever it's called, what other caravan is there to join? Besides, in Scots, one has no background, except what is very far back indeed, no background of poems, I mean, except for H. MacDiarmid, who is not to be followed; and the effect on me is that I hardly write two poems running in the same style, which seems a weakness. Also it explains somewhat why I find it so very difficult every time. It seems to me I have a lot to learn, or rather, to hear about. I mean, I don't know any trigonometry, but at least I know there is such a thing, whereas in poetry there must be a lot to know that I haven't even heard of. Could you advise, next time we meet?

PS: I wish I could answer P. Valérie back anent his bit in *Adam* about London Bridge. I am one of *cette foule* every day.

Note: In 1954 an article on Garioch by Ian Fletcher appeared in *Chanticlere* I, 4, a magazine edited by Patrick Galvin. The main part of that article is as follows:

29

...Born in 1909, Garioch began writing during his years at Edinburgh University. "These first poems," he tells us, "were in the speech I used in the street as a boy; but not," he adds, "at the Royal High School." His work is mainly fugitive. For, though he writes with all the technical rigour of one in the true "Makar" tradition, he is quite casual about the finished material, never disposing of it to magazines unless personally requested. In an idle moment, so it seems, he has collected two little books together: *Seventeen Poems for Sixpence* (1940) — which reached a second edition — and *Chuckies on the Cairn* (1948).

The poems in the earlier book are nostalgically full of the pathos and humour of the Scottish urban scene. They evoke something of the atmosphere of that moving amateur film, *The Singing Street*, where the spirit of the city expresses itself through the singing games of the children with their grave ritual movements. In *Fi-Baw*, for example, Garioch writes of the game as it is played in back streets and of the children's great enemy "the Gayfield polis."

The language of this volume is, like its subject matter and its emotional range, somewhat constricted, while the *Chuckies on the Cairn* is filled mainly with occasional pieces, typical among them a wry reflection on the Festival from the point of view of a native of Edinburgh.

Much of the work written immediately after the war remains uncollected, or unpublished. Still uncollected is Garioch's tribute to Robert Fergusson, the precursor of Burns. Written in the metre first used by Robert Sempill of Beltrees in the seventeenth century, and handled with such frequent skill by Fergusson himself, the metre of *Holy Willie's Prayer*, Garioch's poem is not only a technical *tour de force*, both metrically and in diction, but an example of creative criticism in verse. It should have an automatic right of entry to any anthology covering the last twenty or thirty years.

More recently, Garioch has concentrated on widening the scope of his work, both in subject-matter and in vocabulary. We may regret the disappearance of earlier enchanting themes — of the mystery, melancholy and humour of Edinburgh; of the narrow yet vigorous life of her streets; but this is amply compensated for by the skill and dignity of the later writing. Much of it is translation, but translation in so richly personal a manner acquires the authority of original work. Not less remarkable is the tact Garioch reveals in selecting originals that accord with his limitations. A "hamely" man himself, he frankly disclaims much knowledge of the languages he prefers — Italian, Latin, Greek. Yet, for the most part, his versions reproduce with lively fidelity the spirit of their originals. Here is a stanza from a Pindaric fragment, in which the Greek poet mocks gently at his own ornate style, and suits his tone to his subject-matter — the courtesans of the Great Mother — "Corinthian Aphrodite's sacred hures."

> Your daywerk is the amber tears to brenn
> o frankincense in reekie sacrifie
> and oftentimes ye ettle, fidgin-fain,
> to birl in tourbillons o ecstasie
> abune the beryall firmament on hie
> whaur luve concentrat bleezes til a sterne
> and preclair Aphrodite reigns superne...

Notice the sly "daywerk," the tension established between the aureate diction, typical of Middle Scots — "preclair," "beryall," "superne," magnificent for use wherever ritual solemnity is demanded — and the brisk words from common speech: "reekie," "ettle," "birl," to say nothing of the Burnsian "fidgin-fain." (Equally, Garioch is capable of inventing delightfully expressive words, such as "snishit-snashit" from his translation of one of the *Carmina Burana*.) The total effect is that, while the oriental lusciousness of the temple service is vividly depicted, the scene

30

remains massively anchored in day-by-day reality by an infusion of colloquialisms. Garioch does not cheapen Pindar's language, nor does he make it remote. There is, of course, in Scotland a tradition of placing the Classics in local idiom among a local *mise-en-scene*; "Horace in Home-spun." To the humour and topicality of this tradition, Garioch adds the ability of transmitting the tone of his original. Here, for example, is an anonymous Sicilian serenade of the thirteenth century transformed into his contemporary dialogue between a gudewife and her lover in the street below.

[There follows a quotation of "A Wee-bit Nicht-music."]

Garioch's recent work culminates in a majestic translation from Hesiod. Here, he is dealing with a primitive but powerful original and with a subject traditionally familiar to Scots poets — winter. The diction dense but sinewy, at once archaic and homely, reveals just how far his resources of language have developed since the days of *Seventeen Poems*.

> In Februar come foul days, flee them gin ye may,
> wi' their felloun frosts, days that wad flype an ox,
> whan Boreas blaws owre Thrace, whaur they breid capillis,   *horses*
> and brulyies the braid sea, and gars it blawp;
> and the winterous yird and the woddis warsle aathegither...

The shaggy alliterative metre, an exact equivalent for the "Boetian" hexameter, recalls Dunbar's *Tua Marrit Wemen and the Wedo*, while the scene itself might well derive from one of the Prologues to Gawain Douglas's *Aeneid*. If we scrutinise the vocabulary, we shall find its total effect amounts to something of a throw-back to the times of James III and IV, when Middle Scots was at its most gnarled; when the political ties between England and Scotland were at their loosest. A redacted version of the whole passage was recently given by the B.B.C.

In sum, it can be said that Garioch is strong in the formal set piece and above all in the creative discipline of translation. We can look forward with confidence to many masterpieces of our European inheritance appearing in Lallans for, with his touch of pathos and humour, for sensing and embodying the tone of his models, Garioch has fitted himself for this task supremely well. Other names in the Scots literary scene may glitter more than his, but no-one now is doing more to enlarge and diversify the existing richness of the Lallans tradition than Robert Garioch.

[To J. K. Annand]   1 Sept 55

Thank you for the 2/6, for the *Chuckies* and *17 Poems*, which I duly send. There aren't many copies left now, and most of them are not altogether pristine, but I picked out the two best. One of these days I shall get out a proper book with cloth covers, but when, I don't know.

I keep working away, slowly. Finished translating George Buchanan's *Jephtha* into Scots, and the next thing to tackle is his *Baptist*. When the two are finished, shall try to publish them together. I offered *Jephtha* to the Glasgow BBC and Glasgow Citizens' Theatre, but they voted against performing it. All the same, it is a fine dignified tragedy, not long enough for a whole evening, that might well be followed by a short comedy and make a theatrical outing that might attract an audience. However, I daresay they all know best.

There seem to be some young? chiels coming on who can write in Scots. Edward Boyd manages it with what seems like ease. Don't know about Iain Crichton Smith; shall get his book. What about Edith Anne Robertson? Must find out. George Todd seems good. It's still not fizzling out, anyway. What about yoursel? I'm out of touch, badly; a pity but that can't be helped, I think.

PS: If you have time, what about dramatising some of W. E. Aytoun's stories in *Blackwood's*? I did one: *Dreepdaily Burghs*, duly rejected by BBC. But still think somebody could do something about these things.

[*To J. K. Annand*] 1 Oct 55

...Surely you will get hospitality in *Lines Review*, a good institution, especially now that Smith is its heidmaister. He has livened it up a good deal already. Do you foregaither with Smith? You should, though you probably do in any case. The Edinburgh makars are a lively lot, and you should be one of them if you're not. I've given up looking for bottom-room in the *Saltire Review*, and now deliberately prefer *Lines Review*.

But it is an awful strain, this Deacon Brodie sort of life, Sutherland by day and Garioch by night, schoolmastering and making poetry being such different things, and yet both tiring you out in the same way, that's the damn thing about it. So for the last fortnight I've had a kind of revulsion or scunner and can't bear to read or write or do anything serious in the evenings. Usually I'm half-gyte with the thought of so much to do and only the evenings to do it in, so that the day seems an irrelevant and maddening interruption, however quietly it may be got through; 10 lines done between 7 and 9, and pick it up again next evening at 7. What a life.

Surely the Burns Prize should not damn you in the view of the long-haired boys. I'm one of them myself, though most of the hair has been pulled out in tufts long ago. They're all trying to write Scots the best way they can, and do you realise that you and I belong to about the last age-groups to have spoken Scots as laddies in the ordinary way of life? I'm not sure, but I fear that must be about true, at least in places like Edinburgh. Perhaps not. But the great thing is that they keep on trying. Have you met Tom Scott?...He toils very sedulously in Scots, having deliberately changed over from English. There must be some younger fellows, but I don't know them. But you should meet Tom Scott and discuss things. This resurrected word *Lallans* surprised me when I came home from the war, but the accompanying activity surprised me even more, and there seemed to be the exciting atmosphere that we never used to have. (This, too, just when I moved to London; for a complication of reasons I couldn't bear to come back to Edinburgh, so got a job in London on coming out of the army and here I am.) But I don't care much what it is called, so long as there is interest, which there never was very much of before the war, or so I excuse myself for wasting such years of time, and now I try to make up for it. But I find it very hard to get onto a clear line of development, and keep writing in different styles. All the same, so did Milton, and no 17th-century poet could have been at all pleased if told he could be recognised by his style. It is hard to decide even on one's vocabulary for the purpose of a particular poem.

Do you know, I think I'm inclined to start Lallans-bashing again, to-morrow, 7-9 pm. We shall see....

[To Hamish Henderson]   2.10.55

...I shall try to listen to your programmes from Scotland. We can just manage to hear the Scottish Regional, with luck, after dark, by putting extra voltage on the filaments, which is brutal, but works. Our wireless is ancient, 3-valve, straight circuit, so that it is remarkable to hear the Scottish Regional at all. I shall have a good try, anyhow.

I've already become a member of the Auk Society, and impatiently await my free copy. That's one thing to be interested in, anyhow.

Note: On the same sheet we read:

Do you use the Scottish Style Sheet for spelling? It seems a good idea. I have tried to keep to it since it came out. It is given again in *Lines Review* No. 8 or 9, I forget which.

These three sentences are scored out, and the following added:

(This was meant for a letter to Jimmie Annand. Do you know him?)

[To J. K. Annand]

Dear Jamie,
   I was richt weill-pleisit
to read your scrieve in words weill-cheisit
whan in the morn mysel I'd heisit
   frae beddy-baw;
it's seenil that I'm that ameisit
   sae near day-daw.

Sometime about the hinner-end
o August, I've a mind to spend
a week or twa amang the kenn'd
   Edinburgh faces —
whilk, better nor your ain, can lend
   the toun some graces?

I dout I've taen an awfy time
to say I'll gie your phone a chime
and dram wi ye, & gae hame syne
   on scaffy's barry — och,
it's taen sae lang to find a rhyme
   for —
     Yours aye,
      Garioch

[To J. K. Annand]

...I see jobs are advertised in primary schools in Fife, and have ½ a mind to move there and live in Dunfermline. The Fife committee, however, I seem to remember, always had a bad name. What do you know? All this very tentative: I've been thinking about this for a long time, and have done nothing. Somewhere near Edinburgh, I always fancy. But it's an upheaval unpleasant to think of, with children at school an aa. We'll see. But perhaps you will tell me what the labour market is like for teachers (Chap. III). One great advantage of London, and, in fact, of England, is that they don't bother about these categories, and if you can do the job that's all they are concerned with. However, I'm getting tired of foreign parts, now that the sojourn in London has served its purpose....

[To J. K. Annand] 16 Nov 57

Monie braw thanks for your postcard with the very fine picture. If you hadn't suggested it I should not have thought of sending a poem to the *Scotsman*. Also thanks for looking into the question of Fife. I've sent for application form for Bo'ness Academy: live in Linlithgow or somewhere. Probably no chance of that job, wanting 2nd class Hons., and having not even Article 39, but only a thing caad Article 55 or something of that sort.

But now appears in the *Scotsman* an advertisement for a man & wife job in a school on one of the islands of Orkney! And both my gude wife and I seriously thinking of applying for that. The roll of the school is 17. Now one principal reason why this present school of mine is becoming less of a delight is that the roll is presently going to be 1,100, and not 1,100 of the choicest of Hackney either, as it will become less selective though always made up of many of the Chosen People, of walit folk as Jephthah would put it (and I've started the process of publishing *Jephthah & Baptist* at my own cost, by the way). I'd rather have liked to buy a new motey-car with the money, but then there may be no roads on this island anyhow. Certainly, one might transfer from Hackney to Kent or somewhere, but it does seem time to go to Scotland (if they will hae me, which Edinbro, sweet Edinbro, won't). So Fife & West Lothian & East Lothian of much interest. But Orkney very well worth considering. The children might not be pleased, but on the other hand they might, and it couldn't be helped anyhow if they did not.

[To a Friend] 10 May 58

I have applied for a job in Midlothian, and I hear they have been making enquiries in Kent, so there must be some chance. I hope it will come off. It is more or less now or never, as we've just realised, owing to the dates of the usual big events in our children's schooling: the girl's G.C.E. etc. Hence the sudden haste, which is a bit extraordinary after twelve years or so. Of course they may not want my services: we'll soon see.

11 June 58

. . . Yes, I still have a notion that I could be a Scottish teacher in a Scottish school, but schools are michtie difficult places. I've got

35

that Saltire pamphlet "Scotland in the Schools." But I'm tired of being split in about three, and it's bad for anyone, and maybe that's one reason why the poetry has dried up lately. They tried to anglicize us somewhat in the Royal High School in my day, keeping to the 18th-century tradition, but things seem to be different now. Hector MacIver is turning out a whole generation of R.H.S. boys interested in Scottish literature.

[To Ian Fletcher] (?1958-59. *Not long after the move to 4 Nelson Street*)

... Yes, more cribs from Carne-Ross would be very helpful. I don't officially know Italian, and the Romanesco just about baffles me altogether. There seem to be very few (no) books in English about Belli. The National Library here has the books catalogued by authors, so there may be books lurking somewhere that I haven't found. But they have many catalogues and book lists belonging to other concerns, and in none of them could I find anything under *Belli* or *Romanesco*, or even under *Italian Literature*, which I wanted. I suspect that the books do not exist at all. Shall try Clark, Eleanor, however. It seems to me a book about Belli in English would be worth somebody's while to write.

Very pleased to hear of your meeting with MacDiarmid. He is indeed very civil in good company....

[To a Friend] 16 October 60

The reports of the English critics of the *Wallace* showed how successful Smith had been with his propaganda. The facts that it was performed as the centre-piece of the Festival, and went off with such a bang, and attracted increasing houses all the time, make it a triumph, sure enough. Edward seemed all right. The big danger in that play was that Edward might overshadow Wallace, and I think Smith managed the last act very well: a difficult job, because the court found Wallace guilty, and he comes out on top in the play. But it is a frightful story: not surprising that my wife hated it, and came out horribly impressed. Ian said it was a "smasher." I couldn't quite discover what Helen made of it.

We listened to the play on the wireless shortly after we came here, when Ian was struggling with the history as taught in his new school. Some weeks later, a question on the Battle of Stirling Bridge turned up in an exam, and he answered it all wrong, because he thought this battle was invented in the imagination of Sydney Smith.

[To Ian Fletcher]   21.9.61

. . . I went back to the Epstein show on the extra week, when it was not so crowded, and discovered that the Oscar Wilde tomb had a representation of a wing on the top part. I had got the plot all wrong the first time: thought the figure was in a place like a coal-mine, I having taken his wings for a slab of rock he was squeezed under, somehow.

I got a lot of pleasure out of the R.S.A. exhibition (not the R.S.A. part of it, however).

[To a Friend]   8 November 61

I like being in Edinburgh, and I like meeting the literary boys, who are to be found in a strictly limited set of howffs. Not much visiting at houses seems to go on, instead one mills about in a crowd, getting a word in here and there. There is a good deal of sojourning to Callum Macdonald's late at night of a Friday: he is very robust in his hospitality, and that says a lot for him: he works on Saturdays. Every time I have been there, things were still going strong when I left, and that was late enough. It is a nice walk home over the Meadows in the morning. N. MacCaig mostly presides everywhere, as is his due. S. Smith is to be seen here and there. He has written a new play, but I don't think anyone has seen it yet. T. Scott did very well in Hons. Eng. . . . Scott Moncrieff is in America meanwhile. There is an interesting woman who lives down the road from us, in Fettes Row: J. McGuffie. She wrote to me c/o *The Scotsman* and we were both amused, because she had been teaching in the same school as myself but neither knew of the other's interest in poetry. She wants to publish poetry, and has started doing it too, beginning with Ian H. Finlay, whom I went round to meet; a good chap but very nervous in some way, and not able to go out in the street in daylight. Some of his poems are very good indeed, as it seems to me, but he is liable to be offended if editors do not think they are all good, which of course they don't. There was a poetry-reading ploy, with which these people were connected, in a deep and dark cellar in North St Andrews Street, where I went and read *Embro to the Ploy* beneath a wee light to a lot of shadowy figures who laughed loudly at the funny bits, and it was good fun, but I can't tell you who they all were, as it was too dark. This seems to have been a Festival ploy, as the cellar is always closed when I pass now. A curious business, with poetry mixed up with jazz and various other things that seem incompatible. Someone announced a forthcoming event at which Somebody would be swingin his poems. Critical judgment on my effort was that the audience had been *sent*, i.e. had enjoyed the performance. Well, that's O.K. by me, though I think this expression is out of date. Queer business, altogether. Also there is a good deal of guitar-playing and singing of Scottish folk music as it is called, with Hamish Henderson stirring it all up in great style. Trouble with me is that I can no longer stand the guitar three-chord-trick (tonic, dominant, subdominant). I greatly enjoy the playing of Segovia, so it can't be the instrument that gives me the jim-jams.

...These cellars take up half the area of the house, partly underground, and make a fine workshop. This house gives us much pleasure, though it is a queer house too, and turned out to be complete with dry rot as well as woodworm, but we have had those attended to. A bad business that reminds me of, reported in today's *Scotsman*, that St George's Church in Charlotte Square, which was being treated for dry rot, turns out to be in danger of collapse, the weight of the dome pushing out the pillars. £86,000 to put it right! And the trouble is that many people would be very pleased if it did fall down, so as to make a fine space through which to drive their motor-cars. Now the West End traffic organisation, if you can call it that, is all to be changed once more, with poliss instead of lights. The Empire Theatre is to be pulled down, and the Lyceum, and there is to be a grand and useless opera house, and the fine facade of the Synod Hall is to be pulled down and someone hopes to make a lot of money by putting up offices instead, and money is to be made by somebody knocking down St James's Square and putting up a cigar-box skyscraper on the TOP of the HILL. I'm sorry about the Euston portico (why do they call it an arch? A Greek arch?). But I grow gloomy over all this and had better stop....

[To Ian Fletcher]   30.10.63

. . . We recorded ten Edinburgh sonnets and I see they are billed for some day: the last week of October on the Third Programme. I took the chance of acknowledging my introduction to Belli by yourself and Carne-Ross. The other interesting thing is that *New Saltire* did in fact publish *The Muir*, which must surely have made some noise in the world as a result, though I did not hear any, or rather, only little. There have been no more sonnets except one, a recipe for brewing, which is at least a very sound recipe. . . .

[To Maurice Lindsay]   8.11.65

Here are the proofs, which are very good, except for "Ghaisties," which gives me some dismay, as these are not misprints of the present compositor. This is an early published version, and I have since brought my spelling into line with the Scots style-sheet, e.g. not *aw*, but *aa*, which I have corrected, and a few others which I thought could be let go. But I *never* used apostrophes for *an = and*, or *o = of*, etc. I used to write them *an* and *o*. Now I think it best to spell them as in English, knowing that the reader will not pronounce the final letter. But in the early days, compositors *would* correct my spelling to bring it in line with the old-fashioned style, which now looks very old-fashioned indeed. So I used to beg them to follow copy and sometimes they did not even then. These things do not seem to happen nowadays.

I have corrected everything, and hope it is not asking too much. It just won't do as it is.

A wee joke about this poem: somebody chose to read it some years ago on the wireless, this youthful work, and we received it loud and clear. My wife said: "Beware what thou sayest in secret, lest it be shouted upon the house-tops." But that's all in the business.

(It's a damn good love poem, just the same, though not my line nowadays.)

P.S.: I wonder if Sisyphus could be set with a narrower margin, so that each verse could be got into one line, or are my requests becoming too outrageous altogether?

Note: "Ghaisties," "Sisyphus" and "Elegy" were included by Maurice Lindsay in his *Modern Scottish Poetry* (Faber, 1966).

[To J. K. Annand]   23 Feb 66

Bethankit for your wee letter. I got the words of that poem from
the text of *Carmina Burana* as set to music by Carl Orff, which we
learned when we sang it owre the wireless in the Goldsmiths' Choral
Union in or about 1956. I just took it as I found it. But your two
stanzas of translation make it complete. If ever I get out a Collected
Gurks, maybe I may, wi your permissioun & due acknowledgment,
put in yours as weill. Your style and mine not dissimilar, in fact, I
could claim to belong to the Stockaree or Stinkaroo school.

Rumboat Beerioch

Note: the translation referred to is in *Complete Poetical Works*, p. 103, and
see also note on p. 291.

[To Hamish Henderson]   12.12.66

...I don't know, but I wonder if the victims of the Clearances had
got to the stage where they did not care very much any more,
having been so knocked about, and let down by the only people
they should have been able to trust, and especially having lost their
social organisation (as we largely have done, at close range, at
least). I have read of tribes of Indians who just dwindled though in
no specially difficult situation, because they have lost their way of
life that made sense to them.

I don't know if the northern Highlanders were so hard hit by the
45 etc as those further south. Are the men of Caithness and
Sutherland not different, in any case?

Note: The pamphlet was a short article by HH on the Clearances, published in *The
Scots Magazine* in 1966; a longer version appeared in *Cencrastus* in 1980; and an
even longer version is in *The Celtic Consciousness*, ed. Robert O'Driscoll
(University of Toronto Press, 1981).

[To Sydney Tremayne]   3 Aug 67

I am going to send you a Bartok record to play of an evening. It
is not new, but is in good order. It is a string quartet. He has some
rustling and chirping bits that should suit well to be played in a
house in the middle of a wood.

I am not doing much, and my cupboard has been bare for some
time. But here is one verse to be added to The Ploy:

I truly hope we'll try and please
our guid Lord Provost Brechin,
and burn yon film of "Ulysses"
(I've read the buik, a dreich ane)
wi miles of bleizan celluloid,
a hunder pipers screichan,
and effigies of Dr Freud,
and fountains of free skeechan
                    (jist a copy)
at Embro to the ploy.

You may not have heard the exciting news that our City Fathers
(the very name seems improper in this connection) have decided not
to allow the showing of the film of *Ulysses*. (I nearly went to see it
in London, but the seats were aafie dear.) Anyhow, Lord Provost
Brechin (him at's so keen on the Commonwealth Games that we're
no willin to pey for) said in a speech that this film should be burnt
in public (by the public hangman? No, they haven't got one now).
But a whole film on fire would be a fine happening, would it not?

[To Sydney Tremayne]   29 Sep 68

...I have become interested in Apollinaire, in my usual haphazard
manner.... I really did pay attention to this extraordinary poet,
who was being 1968ish about the year I was born. But he was surely
too worried about not getting old-fashioned, i.e. not introducing
new ways. I wonder if the habit of mind caused by science and
machinery, which much concerned him, does not make people
think too much in terms of Mk I and Mk II.

[To Sydney Tremayne]   28 Sep 69

...Here is this one ["Programme Notes," *Complete Poetical
Works*, p. 8], the only recent poem, written specially for those
cynical poetry readings, and in fact it is very interesting to try it. I
have given it three airings, once at a Peace in Vietnam concert run
by people who seemed to think more of Victory than of Peace, and
twice at the Traverse Theatre during the Festival. Sure enough,
each time so far the audience has demonstrated its solidarity with a
knowing chortle about the little wooden crosses and clapped hands
at the counter-revolutionary (I suppose, in their terms) ending.

41

[To a Friend]   28 September 69

They are going to perform Berlioz' *Grande Messe Des Morts* on
the wireless at one o'clock. I shall listen with some anxiety, because
in a new poem (enclosed) ["Programme Notes"] I say it has four
brass bands, and now wonder if I'm thinking of the so-called
Symphony of a Thousand that I heard once in the Albert Hall. It
certainly had four brass bands. Perhaps Berlioz' Requiem has, also.
That poem was written specially for a poetry-reading I agreed to
take part in on behalf of Peace in Viet Nam, which cannot be
anything but a good cause, one would think, but I have doubts if
the committee are not more interested in victory: not quite the same
thing. Anyhow this poem has been trotted out a few times at these
B-Echelon Avant Garde functions at which I appear, and certainly
it is interesting to read it to an audience that likes to be amused by
cynicism, and note their reactions as the attitude shifts. These
poetry-readings now make me want to be naughty, same as I used
to feel in Kirk-hall concerts in aid of the fabric fund. I may have
learned a good deal, but didn't enjoy it at the time, being expected,
or taken for granted, at concerts in Mill's Kirk in Leith, between Gt
Junction Street and Sheriff Brae. The stonework of the front of
that kirk was of some cheap stone that was crumbling away, and
they had concerts every Saturday night to put it right. Now I see it
as bad as ever, so my sufferings were in vain. Maybe not, though:
that repair-job has lasted 45 years or a bit more, I suppose it must
be, as by the time I was 15, I would have rebelled, most likely....

P.S. Sure enough, that Requiem has 4 brass bands. They are
introduced in the "Tuba Mirum."

[To David Black]   26 Nov 69

...I am always very pleased to have an excuse for a trip to London,
and am much, no, greatly, beholden to you for arranging this. Also
I should like to visit Mrs and Mr Squires, both now I think of
Brighton University. I used to be very fond of Brighton, and would
go there to recover from The Dumps. There is a picture of George
IV in the Pavilion that I find more enjoyable to look at than
anything by Rembrandt. I forget who it is by. Have you found that
curious pub under the station, I think it is? And that one full of

sailors on the lower part of the promenade? I remember I once went there on Hogmanae.

Here is or rather are two copies of the *Selected Poems*: better to buy them from me, because that is the only way I can get any money from them, by buying wholesale and selling them retail. I rise up and call you blessed. I shall add for nothing, on second thoughts, a copy of the unwanted *Jephthah*. Jehovah knows I have plenty of copies of that, my favourite work. I read in The Traverse on Saturday night one passage from one of the choruses; the hypocrite and his conscience from *The Baptist*, I think, and was so pleased when a young woman asked me where she could get a copy. I love that book better than the *Selected Poems*.

Here is a still, small invoice:

to 2 copies SELECTED POEMS at 15s.	£1.10.0
Plus postage, whatever the parcel is going	3/-

to cost, according to the stamps stuck on
and you get the smell of Glen Grant
13 yrs old from the gum on the stamp
thrown in for nothing.

Note: the reading referred to was organised by DB at Chelsea School of Art.

[To a Friend]   2 February 70

...A fortnight ago they put me in an armchair in the TV studio they have just set up in the old Gateway Theatre, which was Pringle's Picture House when I was a boy: we used to go to their penny matinees, or rather, most of the boys went, but I was more likely to go to the Picturedrome at the top of Easter Road, where my mother played the piano, and I got in for nothing. Anyhow, I read some poems into the machine, and was duly photographed in movement. My wife Peg and I went on Friday to see the playback, and all I can say about what I saw of myself is that I had better be a lot brisker the next time, if there is a next time. Had I been a stranger, looking on (was I not, in fact?) I would have wished this fellow to get a move on, and not be so annoyingly at his ease, with all the time in the world. That, apparently, is Lesson One to those who try to entertain the public: get on with the job!

[To a Friend]   15 February 70

...I liked the Chelsea students, and they gave me a good hearing, and did their best with the poems in Scots. That Chelsea trip did not need much preparation, but I am a bit troubled over having taken on an invitation to talk to a Burns Club here on Thursday. I am not a speaker or a lecturer or a scholar, and should stick to the one thing I can do, but when they asked me to do this I was full of an idea of Burns as a national hero, having got it into my head that he must have filled an empty space after the military defeat of 1745, which must have been pretty evident still, when Burns began to be known. But I have found this hard to prove and now think it is a wrong idea after all. Certainly the '45 was so complete a victory for the United Kingdom's supporters that they do not seem to have thought it necessary to be very hard on the Jacobites after the post-Culloden massacres were over. Scott brings this out well in *Redgauntlet*. But the Jacobites were in fact the Scottish Nationalists, so patriots like Scott were in a strange position, also James Hogg about the same time, with his Jacobite songs, which were safe to compose, because politically they were significantly finished and harmless. But what about this in Burns' day? (Allan Ramsay was enough of a Nationalist and a Jacobite to have his house knocked down by cannon balls from Edinburgh Castle while the Jacobites were in Holyrood, and their army just out of range.) Burns was so interested in songs that he collected/composed both Whig and Tory songs. But Jacobins provided the serious questions in his day, not Jacobites, and Burns was as Jacobin as a man with domestic responsibilities could very well be, and his Scottish Nationalism was general and safe enough for anyone to follow, or claim to follow. I think still that there is something in this. It is reasonable for anyone to be surprised at such a national love of poetry, or at least of a poet, lasting till this day, when Burns is a hero to many who don't take poetry seriously. There must be something in this, and if I can't do this in a satisfactory way, perhaps I shall be able to ask a few questions that will make it worth the people's while to come out on a cold night. It turns out that only a half-hour talk is expected, and then they go over (thankfully?) to finish the evening with music, so perhaps it will not be too bad after all. All the same, I should have had the sense to tell them I was no speaker, and please, could I read them a few poems instead, which would have been nae bother at aa.

Mr King told me today that you are a lot better.... He came to see me about this anthology.... I like him and admire (wonder at) his energy and enthusiasm, especially for poetry, and wish I had as much, mine happening only when the wind is south-south-east. And this although I have stuck before me a sonnet by Sir William Mure (1593-1657) that starts:

> Look home, my soul, defer not to repent:
> Time ever runs: in sloth great dangers lie.

A curious phrase, "Look home," that comes twice in the sonnet, which is all about getting on with the job in a secular manner, I think. Sam MacLean has been in Edinburgh, an important event, in fact, and he has been going over a tape-recording made at that sit-in in Aberdeen, which we [i.e. *Scottish International Review*] are going to publish. Also he has given us a new poem. He is very seriously concerned with poetry, but little interested in setting it before the public; I mean, that just does not seem to be in his mind much, or even at all, and he sort of sympathises or sadly agrees with people who keep asking him for poems. I think of him and of George Davie, whom he often talks about, as being the two notable young people in Edinburgh in 1932 or so, who will later be thought about as we think about their counterparts in the early 19th century or so. Who do you think? And yet both, I think, work somewhat in a state of despair. Perhaps I am wrong, and am only seeing them through my own visors. But I wonder if we all have a feeling of things falling about our heads. This afternoon I went to the exhibition in the Town Planning Department in the old *News* office, to see the model of the motorway they are about to build. And I wonder how much the ratepayers have to pay for that bloody great model, all made up of paper buildings set on a great map of Edinburgh, with ominous bits of map left at the margins, where this road just stops and leads into no particular street. But I could see that there is nothing of the original Leith Street between Lady Glenorchy's Church and Waterloo Place on each side. I'm even forgetting the names of the pubs they have knocked down. The Harrow Inn, The Register Tap. I forget the other one at the bus station. Pirrie's has gone, and Spiers, opposite it, is closed. The wee pub in Little King Street is gone, and I don't even remember its name, where there used to be the chorus girls etc from the Theatre Royal, now all gone. But I'll be damn sorry when they destroy the Black Bull, where Sydney "gat her." They can have Rutherford's and the Argyle. And they will, anaa. But apart from that, the Cumberland in Cumberland Street (called after the Butcher, not the county, I think) is now The Tilted Wig. I went there once and they charged me 1/7 for a half pint of some commercial beery wash. Not as good as that which now I drink, at 4d per pint, of my own cooking. The best practice nowadays is to have a wee midwife's bag, or, I mean a wee bag as formerly associated with midwives, as in *Ulysses*, where 5(?) cockles rolled. Anyhow, a bag, with a supply of proper beer made at home. You go out for company, and perhaps to the Canny Man to view the go-go-girls, and order a half pint of their prohibitive wallop. (I think you can no longer buy a poney as in the 30s.) This you keep on topping up with viable (excuse me) beer from the grassroots (excuse me) out of your midwife's bag. A whole evening out for 1/7, except for the now prohibitive bus-fare. But it is possible to walk from Nelson St to the Canny Man, and of course nobody would think of coming from the Canny Man to Nelson St by any other means of moving-about. So despite Harold and his Killjoys, one can flourish like a blackbird. They do, indeed. Thrushes exist, but do not seem so successful. Of course, the blackbird, though vocally gifted, is cousin to the Craw, like Callas. Sure to get on. I myself like starlings above all birds. Last December I was delighted to hear the wheeple of a whawp in George Street at dawn at 9.20 a.m. (Wilson's time). It was a stirkie, of course, I knew fine, and so did he, but what difference did that make?

[To a Friend]   11 December 70

That wood-polishing poem ["Perfect," *Complete Poetical Works*, p. 40] turned out better than I expected, at least it pleases people a good deal at poetry-readings, which is something to go by, though there is a lot more to it, of course. It is easy to follow and repetitive, so easy to take in at one reading. I went to a Nelson Hall concert and admired the gloss that some Corporation painter had got on the panelling, and that started the thing off. I don't really know about polishing and staining wood, but my father knew a lot about it, and there is plenty of information about it in one of his books that is still in the house. He made two violins and varnished them beautifully. One of them is considered to have a pretty good tone, very good, in fact, by people who know....

The Dictionary job goes on also. We got cleaned out of our den like a lot of old-established spiders a fortnight or so ago, so that the painters could smarten it up. The other three rooms were not difficult, but the fourth has pigeon-holes nearly to the ceiling on two walls, and books on the other two.... There are 212 of these pigeon-holes, and in each was a pile of slips of paper with words and quotations etc. They all had to be moved into the next room, tied in bundles and labelled. That was the office-boy's job. I am the office-boy. Now the place is all bright and clean and I am moving the slips back in again and sticking labels on the dookits as one of the painters called them. Those piles of slips, or a lot of them at least, were quite extraordinarily dusty, so I'm dusting them and putting them in polythene bags, all neat.

[To a Friend]   21 July 71

I am glad you saw that TV show [BBC2, 11 June 71]. I thought a lot of Gavin Millar, who produced it. I very much liked the scenes in Canongate Churchyard, which they did under difficulties, by electric light, because it was a very dull day, in March, I think it was. The electric light very likely gave more interesting effects than sunshine would have given. In the house he would have no room but the kitchen: I wanted to be grand and have it in the genuine Regency Drawing Room, but he liked my wife Peg's yellow and red kitchen. She was away from home at the time...so she was not here to be worried about the house and how it would look. In fact it was not very clean or tidy but it looked all right in the picture. Everybody thinks that was a BBC worm specially placed in the area for the sake of that poem, but it appeared just at the right time out of that crack between the stones. It was pink, too, just as the libretto wanted it to be. That is only twice I have seen a worm just there. I expect it felt the vibrations of all these people walking about, and came up to see if it was raining. It is remarkable, all the same, because the area is much deeper than the street. I think it is the original level of the ground, and that all the streets here have been raised on the earth dumped between the area walls on each side of the street, with the coal-cellars under the pavements. They would build the cellars first, with stone arches and a strong back wall, and dump the earth afterwards. A lot of London is done in the same way, around Bloomsbury and places built about the same period.

[To a Friend] 22 September 71

...The one I think most of in this set [i.e. *The Big Music*] is "The Big Music" itself, and that is the outcome of a visit to a piping competition, it certainly was before 1959, plus an interest I began to have in Piobaireachd (as I *will* spell it, for all the world as though I spoke Gaelic). But the trouble was that I knew nothing about it, and could not tell at what point the tuning-up gave place to the tune. However, I got a piping record, and a BBC book, and felt brave enough to risk the rage of the pipers....

I am assured by people who really know that "Ceol Mor" means Big Music as distinguished from Small Music, i.e. dances and marches. It has not the special meaning of Great, which we all use too much and far too loosely. I think "The Big Music" is more of a success than "The Muir," which is too difficult an attempt altogether, but still is a pretty good try, all the same.

[To J. B. Caird] 1 Oct 71

Here at last is my little book [*The Big Music*], which I am so pleased to send you. I have to agree that although Mr Humphries has taken a long time about it, he has produced a very decent-looking job at a price that knocks out most other books of this size. For although he has only 54 pages, he does manage to get a lot of material into them, without the thing looking overcrowded, and I find his type quite readable, whatever artistic people may say, and it is clean and free from hairiness and broken bits. He is confused about the use of underlines and quotes, caused partly by lack of italics, but never mind. I have of course immediately spotted some literal misprints that I missed on the proofs.

Peg and I were talking about Robert Duncan, whose book I fetched out for another despair-making look (does it remind me of those early Apocalyptics?). Peg said she liked him when he came, and still had a clear picture of what he looked like. She said it seemed he thought the whole of our country was disconcertingly small, and that we in 4 Nelson Street seemed disconcertingly placid. He seemed to find America overwhelmingly big, however. Then we both agreed that we have moved very little about Britain, or even Scotland, and that reminded me of a thought I often have, that you must know as much of Scotland as almost anybody, not only geographically, but anent the people, including the children, including the Gaelic-speaking people. And we both thought what we had thought before, that you might write a book about Scotland, not an Anatomy, but a description of the place as inhabited by live people, and the things that keep them alive, materially and spiritually/culturally (I was going go put an *and* between those two adverbs and realised in time how wrong that would be). I daresay you have thought of this yourself, but both Peg and I thought that if we suggested it, you might consider it as having seconders as well as a proposer. You know the Borders too, do you not? Not Fife, perhaps? I would suggest that you leave out the parts you don't know well. The parts you do know well would be enough to be going along with. Because I marvel myself at the bigness of even Scotland. Looking down Dundas Street, as I do often enough, I see on the other side of the Firth a white building on a hillside, and for years I have wondered how far away it was, confused by the shape of the hills as seen from Dundas Street, because the hill to the West has a steep side, like Benarty, which is above Blairadam, where I looked at Adam's umquhile house (the architect, I mean, not the allfather) when Gerald trundled me there in his motor-car, to see the place where a relative of his used to stay. But the house looked nearer than that. Recently I took the train to Burntisland, having seen that on a straight line down Dundas Street you looked straight at a break between the line of trees between Aberdour and Burntisland, and so straight at this house, which indeed in recent years has not been showing up white as it used to do. From Burntisland it turned out to be an easy walk of a few miles, and there was the house, with its whitewash not renewed for a few years. It was hazy over Edinburgh, but Peg and I went there again last Saturday, and we could see or take a sight through the gap in the trees, not clearly and obviously up Dundas Street but the green dome of the insurance office at the corner of George Street and Dundas Street showed up very clearly, and dead in line, the spire (copied from Salisbury) of the Assembly Establishment . . . (there is the Assembly place with two towers by Playfair, artfully lined up with it, so that it seems from Dundas Street to be one building, and did Playfair mean it to be symbolic, or the later architect if he was later, of the Old Tolbooth.) I don't know. But anyway, there it could be seen from the Fifan side. But what I meant to say was that it occurred occured occurred to me that I stand little chance of getting to know that bit of Fife between the Binn and Aberdour, and in any detail worthy of the word, of the country five miles north of those points. So we are in the same plight as the Americans, not to mention the Indians, who have a really big country, and I am trying not to think of the Russians. But the World is not all that big compared with other satellites, or whatever it should be called. Looking at those TV pictures of men on the Moon, it did seem that the Moon is quite big, though we are not in the habit of thinking so. So I would say, and so would Peg (I have just asked her ((I am a great one to verify my statements))) that the Scotland you have personally got to know would be big enough for a biggish book.

University of Edinburgh

SCHOOL OF SCOTTISH STUDIES

17 January 1972

Dear Sir, or Madam, as the case may be,
We request the pleisor of yir companee
At the

21ST BIRTHDAY PAIRTY

of the Schule of Scottish Studies

DRESS INFORMAL, i.e. the usual orra duddies,

ON THE 29TH JANUAR AT 7 P.M.

Sae ye can easy get there efter the gemm.
We'd better tell ye, no to be mair circumstantial,
That ye'll maist likely get something gey substantial,
For, be it said, the Schule of Scottish Studies
Kens mair about cookery than jist hou to byle tatties
                                    and haddies
There's to be Haggis and Clapshot, Stapag, and
                        parritch caad Brochan,
That thick, ye'll maybe can tak some o't hame in yir
                                    spleughan,
Atholl Brose, very nice, to mak yir thochts mair
                                    effervescent,
Frae a genuine Atholl recipe — we mean the Forest, no
                                    the Crescent.

R.S.V.P. BY THURSDAY, 27TH JAN.

Or maybe sometime suiner, if ye can.
And if ye come to

27 GEORGE SQUARE, EDINBURGH

                        frae aa the airts,
Ye'll find parking space fir yir cawrs, caravans and
                                    cairts
Richt forenenst the Schule of Scottish Studies,
And, in the Meedies, guid grazing fir yir cuddies.

51

4, Nelson Street,
Edinburgh 3,
24.1.72

The Schule of
Scottish Studies,

Thanks fir the invite til yir pairtie.
We're keen to come, no on a cairtie,
But in a Twintie-seevin bus;
That will dae weill eneuch fir us.

My wife and I read wi delyte
The letter wi yir kind invite,
And houpe to win, be't wind or weet,
Til this byordinar Schule-treat.

Yours aye,

Robert G. Sutherland.

Note: Mary MacDonald, who worked in the archives of The School of Scottish Studies and who was an old friend of Garioch's, recalls that when the School celebrated its twenty-first birthday Garioch produced, at short notice, the above invitation. The replies, like Garioch's own, were in kind. Mrs MacDonald adds: "He worked in the School over several years transcribing Child Ballads for the Bronson collection. How he enjoyed the various versions from the tinkers and also their tales which he also transcribed. His transcription of Jeannie Robertson's autobiography is quite inimitable. He breathes life into it." She also quotes a limerick he laid on her desk one day:

At Linlithgow, down there by the loch,
Tam Dalziel met a man who said, "Och!
  Mr. Dalyell, but why
  spell your name with a "y,"
and what have you done with your "yoch"?

[To Ian Fletcher]   2 Nov 72

...Pleased to have word of you. I flourish meantime in 2nd year of
2-year incumbency or recumbency as Resident Writer in Edinburgh
University. A quote from Carne-Ross much discussed at a lecture
last week by new professor — Robson — more or less the question
whether or not you need to be a Roman Catholic to read Dante to
advantage....Both Ian and Helen now married and gone
respectively to Kent and Yorkshire. Peg and I have the house to
ourselves and don't entirely like it.

[To Sydney Tremayne]   5 Nov 72

Now to my surprise I find that my output of poetry which has
shrunk as expected, owing to the beneficient perversity of
everything, is not equal to what is expected of me, and I wonder if
this sort of thing explains a lot with regard to those Great Men and
cetera, for now that I am within striking distance of the Old Age
Pen (that fooled you? No: never mind) sion I have no thoughts that
batter at the doors of scansion, in fact I would like to be left quietly
though not forgotten; how absurd!

There is an unfamiliar tendency now in me to be only moderately
pleased when people approach me, except with cheques, though
latterly I have stipulated that my fee for a reading should be paid in
used, train-robber-type notes, more negotiable at face value: a dirty
face is worth more than a clean face; though as things are going I
think I shall in future insist on being paid in the form of a fish
supper, only as I am in considerable demand these days I shall insist
that there be included no fewer than two pickled ingins, onions I
mean....

[To a Friend]   17 December 72

...My university job has been renewed for this year, as I thought it
might be, but couldn't be sure. My successor in October is to be
Sorley Maclean, who has just retired from his job as headmaster of
the Plockton School. They are very pleased at getting his consent to
come to Edinburgh and do this job, and so they may well be. He is
a quite exceptionally fine man, and it will be good for the university

53

to have a Gael.... Sorley comes from a famous family of Macleans, and has a strong awareness of family, which we just don't have. This university job is very interesting, and keeps me pretty busy, in fact, because all sorts of people come to show me what they have written, and to discuss it. In a way, it is quite an important job, for the Resident Writer is outside of the academic life and yet belongs to the staff, which enables him to be quite useful to the students. People have even come from outside the university: last year there was an unemployed young fellow who was writing an immense novel. Now he has become caught up with archaeological digging and has become a working-man, not being too bigoted to refuse a job that he finds interesting.

[To Sydney Tremayne]   18 Dec 72

Here is my "Oil-Strike" [*Complete Poetical Works*, p. 150], not a badly constructed effort, though not much else. However, old boy, as I always say, they can't beat us at construction, haw haw, only nowadays there is this damn thing they call structuring, or whatever damn present participle, I mean verbal noun, they have for it. Well, I mean, this "Oil-Strike" is not badly structured, in its way, I say. And those petrol tins did leak all over the sand. And the Saint Sunniva (Leith to Aberdeen) was all I could afford. And that early novel — a load of tripes, ole boy, full of Social Credit and Antizygy (*sic*), written in those callow days when I still thought Hugh MacDiarmid was a poet at least as good as Eliot and Pound and a Scotsman to boot.

[To Sydney Tremayne]   14 April 73

...I don't want to be known even in W.C.1. as a comic poet. Mind you, I should rather be known as anything than not known, except to the polis, so long as it is on paper; personal notoriety is a consummation devoutly to be unwished. Well, all this is fine, but I wish I had written some or a few poems with that grave controlled humorous quality of so many of those in your *Selected and New*, and to present them to the eye as well as to the ear. That is what I lack: a visual sense. And it is because of the music largely that I like Scots. I could not write to you sooner, because last weekend I had to lecture to or read a paper to a load of professors and such at a very laudable weekend conference or yacketyyack about Scots and its use. And I was worried about this, and spent a lot of time making notes, weeks and weeks, and wrote the whole script out in sentences instead of headings, and read it to the clock and found it would take 65 minutes, which would leave 25 minutes for discussion. And of course when the time came, and I had a platform and a desk and a wee light and a giraffe of water, I began to enjoy myself and abandoned my script and began to blether until the chairman nudged me to say there was only five minutes left for questions and dissection. . . .

Also this week I have or plead that I have had to be where I should/would have been pleased not to be, to listen to Heinrich Böll, born in Naziland against his will, or near Naziland, in 1917, who now describes himself as a tired old man. What about me and you? But I greatly respect him, though too mean to have bought his novels. And I wanted to finish knocking into Scots two Belli sonnets to have them ready for Carla Spadavechia (what a name for a nice young gal — old sword!) when she comes back on Monday for the summer term (we pagans don't observe Easter). And I did. It takes me from one third to two thirds of a day (the day being divided into the spaces between breakfast, dinner, tea and supper) to translate one Belli sonnet. And then there are plenty of second thoughts. What about the last line of No. 272? "buggiarà sto Governo si se sarva." That started as "Whit chance d'ye gie this Government? — fient a hait." Archaic, mannered, unconvincing. This word "buggiarà" is too precious to lose. It occurs often in Belli, meaning destroyed in some way. Second attempt — "The Government is feenisht, oniegait." How absurd. What we want is, "The Government is buggered, oniegait." Or "buggart?" Translating the Eyetie, I would have "buggert."

[*To Sydney Tremayne*]   2 Aug 73

. . .that book [*Doktor Faust in Rose Street*, Macdonald, Lines Review Editions No. 3] was produced with misgivings, and having missed its offered earlier date because I had nothing new to put in, and I kept saying soon I shall have something, but in the end I did not have much, except for some terribly dreary things like "Dreary Circle" — well, it is something I suppose even to express dreariness.

Oh how I hate binary reasoning! It is a very long time since I was surprised to be confronted with this, in Milne's Bar in 1933 or 1934, when C. M. Grieve put it to me was I with him (for him) or against him, and I thought first it was shocking that he should so quote Christ's reported words (confirmed by usually reliable sources) but then was dismayed by the suggestion that I should be either a Communist or a Fascist (i.e. not a Communist). How I hate this kind of thing, which still goes on, even and indeed largely among students, not all admittedly students of logic. That "Dreary Circle" must at least be the dreariest poem as distinct from these merely boring of recent date. It is specially good that you should see good in "Lesson," which had to be written because I suddenly found that one of the Apollinaire translations intended for this barrel-scraping publication had been in *The Big Music*. And I was nae-weill, and wrote that about something that had seemed not very promising. BUT how interesting to compare my poem with those two translations from Apollinaire! How good a poet he thereby appears, and how little I need to be ashamed in his company! For here we are (yes, including I) venturing on to very high mountains.

[To J. B. Caird]   23 Jan 74

...I have been engaged to purvey one rough-and-ready set of verses each week for a commercial wireless company, Radio Forth; its purlieu is from Fife to the Lothians. That is, so long as I can keep it up: that is understood. £5 per week, gross. The prose book from Southside was to be out about now, but is being delayed. I met Robin Lorimer at [Sydney Smith's] funeral, also MacCaig and A. Scott, and Dennis Peploe, whom I had not met for a very long time. And T. Scott also: at one stage I found myself right beside him, and said Hullo in a tentative way. He fixed on me a look of stern disapproval, and was gone. Sorley Maclean was there, the best of all. I came straight home. It was at the Dean Cemetery, I went down the hill to the Flora Stevenson and turned right, buying on my way one regulation-sized bottle of draught sherry for 59p from a shop that was advertising it. Good it was, too. I expect you find it good to be retired. I miss the Dictionary, though. They are down to the two editors and the secretary, I think, unless someone is working for nothing. I have not written any serious poetry lately that was any good, but have at least, I think, seen what was wrong with the failures....

Michael Hamburger was in Edinburgh last week....I didn't
know how he knew me, but he remembered meeting me at George
Fraser's literary evenings, it must have been about fifteen years
ago. That is very remarkable, is it not? He is a very good poet: that
impresses me more and more....It seems that everything about
him has something to do with poetry, or nearly everything to do
with poetry. He gave a very good reading, too, with an appearance
of casualness, but not too much of that. For my part, I like to have
everything ready to look up, and I cannot stand a tenth-rate poet
affecting contemptuous ease and hunting about a bundle of waste
paper, and saying "I'll read this one — no, on second thoughts I
won't!" And another curious experience was to hear his opening
"political" poems, which he said were written rather against the
grain, forced on him by events. Well, my heart sank at first,
because they were so much like so many poems that seem bad to
me, that I have heard in so many seedy joints while waiting my turn
to come on. And I think perhaps they were ordinary poems in the
sense that a lot of wearifully ordinary people can write them just
about the same. But when he rather thankfully gave up reading
those, he went on to be a very good poet indeed, and this isn't a
review I'm writing, thank God! so that's as far as I will go, only I
began to feel my inside full of discomfort, and I haven't felt like
that for a long time since I have been paddling about in so many
shallows, but I remember very well what causes this: it is finding
yourself in the presence of an art that it might perhaps be possible
to join in and swim in, perhaps not!

I was foolishly disappointed in his lecture, which was entitled
"Form and Structure in Poetry." Now I am fascinated and scared
by the relationship between the "subject" of a poem (well, you
know what I mean: it has to be about something, I really think so)
and the metre that is to be used. In music, the music is the subject,
but "sound poetry" is never more than an interesting curio; it must
have a meaning conveyed by the words, after all that is what words
are — sounds that carry a meaning....But he defended free
verse — that was the gist of his lecture — by questioning the existence
of metre, and illustrated this by trying to scan a great many
passages from the Classics in which, though there might be one
iambus, there were never five in an iambic pentameter. So free
verse is not metrical — so what? Neither is blank verse, nor Pope's

heroic couplet for that matter. I do not feel easy about this: it is rather like saying that Burlington House is not really Palladian owing to, etc., therefore the Daily Mirror building opposite Gamage's is no less of a formal piece of architecture. I think in the end he said that free verse was distinguished from prose by being more intensified in meaning. This could not be tolerated in prose, which goes on longer. But surely I have got him wrong. What about an epic, which goes along mainly in not-too-intense verse, but which becomes intense when the time comes for greater intensity. . . .Even ill-tempered neighbours raise their voices in a stair-heid row only when the current of life calls for a special effort of flyting. And, I must say, I can hear an iambic pentameter even in "Tomorrow and tomorrow and tomorrow," which was one of the examples he had chosen at random. I remember very well at school fifty years ago being disgusted and cynical about the metrical scansion that the English and French and Latin masters all tried to apply to classical verses. I could see that it fitted the English lines like a B. Hyam suit, i.e. where it touched. . . .Was not sure about the French, for whom one had to make allowances anyhow, and those ancient Romans seemed all to have been daft — just think of the drivel they wrote! . . . I don't know all that much of Apollinaire, of course, because of the language difficulty, but I can see that often he is being drawn back to the alexandrine and diverging from it, but without this going on he would be writing much more loosely and not so well.

[To Sydney Tremayne]   21 April 74

You showed more fortitude than I did in the face of that second-last *Lines Review*, because I looked at it and saw the Robinson Crusoe piece and the A. Fowler piece and decided each time to read it sometime soon, and then I had to tidy the room as it had got out of hand, and I have not seen that copy since. Professor Fowler was one of my bosses when I was Resident Writer and I found him very agreeable, but I can make nothing of his poetry. That is a familiar experience, however, as it is to find reviewers, etc., praising poetry I can make nothing of, in terms I cannot understand. Robin Fulton is at least trying to make *Lines Review* more interesting. It was a bit repetitive. . . .

Plenty of words keep forming in my head, but all are useless as poem-fodder: grade C3, so much coveted by men of military age in all times. . . .

Yesterday, or the day before, I was driven to West Linton, to the house of Ronald Stevenson, an amazing pianist:

> Mrs Twinkatwank Twunk was a grand pianiste;
> She could make the most wonderful sounds,
> Like the noise of a dozen steam-organs, at least,
> That you hear on the merry-go-rounds.

To give you a dim idea of his pianistic powers, let me tell you that he can and does play the "Fantasia Contrapuntistica" by Busoni. I have heard him do it, and much good it did me!

Well, during my visit he quickly composed a musical setting for my sonnet about R. Fergusson's grave. It is very good indeed, but I wonder if all poets do not altogether quite entirely like it when their poems are musicked by composers, almost certainly more eminent than themselves anyhow, who have their own ideas about the lengths of vowels. A sonnet set to music should have fourteen lines, should it not? I heard R. Stevenson's setting last night on the wireless of a prose passage by Hugh Mac-Guess-Who, and thought that more suitable for musical treatment. But hypocritically or from a mere desire to please, I admired that musical setting, which sure is mighty fine.

Peg says, or rather gently suggests, that my undervaluing of everything is just one of the things expected of an OAP. I shall try to remedy that. I shall start by practising the piano part of Ronald Stevenson's setting of my sonnet. It starts in G flat and quickly goes into C major. How, I don't know. . . .

But the one thing that has truly interested me lately was the preparation of that *kriegsgefangenschaft* book, *Two Men and a Blanket*. I started off in the thirties in prose, with short stories admired by nobody but myself, but here are 80,000-90,000 words of good prose, for which I prepared by buying a copy of *Robinson Crusoe*. And in supplying new bits, I think I did as well as originally in our digs at 30 Antrim Mansions, N.W.3, when Peg and I were happier I think (and so does she) in 1945 than at any time before or since, except for the present. . . .

59

[To a Friend]   23 June 74

I wrote [*Two Men and a Blanket*] in 1946 during my long leave in
the army, just back from gefangenschaft in Germany, and
previously Italy, while it was fresh in my head. I could not interest
any publishers in it, though I tried most of the likely ones. The
book is not about the War, very much, and there are no exciting
escapes. But now Southside are going to publish it — an Edinburgh
publisher — I hope they will not regret it. But they think the time
may be right, now that the excitement of that war is over, and
people are much interested in questions of survival, which is what
this book is about. My word! A thought strikes me. I have come
over with some paper etc to Queen Street Garden, and have it all to
myself (it is rather dull and cold), and just noticed that this garden
is about the same size as our compound in Benevento. What a
curious thought. And I have a key to get out. Anyhow, this book
(100,000 words, nearly) has gone to the printers and the first proofs
are promised "soon." This really is exciting. It is in a kind of
Robinson Crusoe prose. I read that book with care before starting
it, so as to help my prose style. That also counted against it in
1946-47, I think.

Tomorrow I have to go to St Andrews to read some of my poems
at a summer school. That is no worry at all. But in August I have to
go to three schools in Fife on three mornings at 9.30, to give a
lecture to teachers-in-service; it is to be called "Poetry in Schools"
and I am described as writer-in-residence at Edinburgh University,
though that job was over a year ago. And I was a very
undistinguished teacher. A long time ago somebody asked me if I
was interested in this thing, hurriedly, over the phone. I said
perhaps, and wanted to know more about it. Then a long silence,
and the next I heard was that the syllabus arrived, all nicely printed,
and there was my lecture and my name, wrongly spelt, and my
qualifications, a year out of date. A-well, I shall put a bold face on
it, and try to entertain those teachers, sympathising with them for
being inside school buildings in August. But I shall not try to
conceal the fact that they all know more about poetry in schools
than I do.

[*To Sydney Tremayne*] 24 Sept 74

... Very much taken up with antics, some of them rather odd, e.g. reciting poetry in a midden; instructing teachers how to suck eggs; lecturing on Scots poetry to a class of students who hardly understand English, entertaining Aberdeen school scholars (students, I mean, they like to call themselves nowadays) and what an awful afternoon I had today! I really am in a strange kind of pickle, difficult to understand, and yet it would not be pleasant to have nobody take notice of my poetry. But it is none of it new. I do everything or at least a good many of the things associated with poets, except that of writing poetry. But at least I can still manage to think it is funny, rather than irritating or disheartening, to have somebody, as this afternoon it happened, praising a stroke of genius, when I was only using a cliché of the time in an obvious sort of way....

There is a tendency now hereabouts to think of my poems as somewhat akin to Robert Fergusson's, and indeed I have studied his poetry with a hope of learning from him, but I don't want to have too much of this sort of thing, even though I look like getting more money from events to be associated with the bicentenary of his death than he ever got in his day (not sure though: he was much in demand; Burns exaggerated, as he was inclined to do). Anyhow, there is a sort of pious tendency to make me a sort of vicariously rewarded Fergusson: this could easily make me foolish, apart from looking foolish. It is an odd business, not easy to keep in its place, as also is this queer thing that has been happening sometimes lately, where I have to give a lecture to an audience largely of academics. Well, that can be done by being careful to give not much besides what I have found by trying to write poetry in Scots – a curious experience – for what it is worth. That is valid enough, I think... I don't mind being a sort of case for these professors to study if they want to.

[*To a Friend*] 2 February 75

In case you are surprised at the enclosed bit of doggerel, I had better explain that I am contracted to supply and read one such bit of verse each week, so long as I can keep it up, for a commercial wireless station that has just been started here, called Radio Forth.

Also, I don't know if the London papers would take any notice, but General Amin did offer to come and be the king of Scotland. It was a great joke hereabouts, and happened at just the right time for my debut as Poet Laureate to Radio Forth. Also by good luck I had found John Buchan's story of the Mohammedan Scotsman. Anyhow, it's all a bit of harmless fun....

I just thought I would include this optical-illusion poem on the Necker Cube [*Complete Poetical Works*, p.133 and note on pp.303-4], as a curiosity, which I realise is a failure, and I know why, because the treatment is all wrong. I shall have another try. These optical illusions and awkward questions of perception seem as though something could be done with them, but not in this old-fashioned way. I have come to this conclusion on my own, except that I could see that nobody thought much of this one.

Radio Forth Poem 1

BEZONIAN

I shall tell a tale of a potentate from far across the Brine,
A tale that deserves, to tell the truth, a nobler pen than mine;
He brings, now Scotland's skies grow dark, though nights are getting shorter,
An offer of assistance from an unexpected quarter.

He is only a foreign general, this man of whom I sing,
But he's available, we hear, to be our Scottish king,
Supposing we should need one, though that remains to be seen;
At least we've got a volunteer; ye ken fine who Ah mean.

'Twas said long ago of some holy place, not far from Africay,
No infidel had trodden its soil, and safely got away
Until the Sultan gave his word, in 1925,
To let some German scientists get there and back, alive.

They reached that holy city, just by the skin of their teeth,
And there they met a Mohammedan, whose name was Thomas Keith;
"Ah'm pleased to see ye, gentlemen," says he, "jist caa me Tam.
Hae ye oniething aboot ye in the natur o a dram?"

He was only a deserter from the Black Watch, so he said,
Backslider from the Auld Kirk, with a price upon his head.
Scotch industry and prudence, he led them to understand,
Had made him Top Official in that hot and dusty land.

So a simple Black Watch soldier, though not exactly a king,
Was appointed to a post of responsibility that amounted to much the
    same thing.
And this must be a true account, I think you will agree,
Seeing that it was stated by John Buchan, M. A., LL. D.

So, if a Black Watch private, upon that sultry shore,
Could make a useful sort of king, as Tom Keith did of yore,
We might return the compliment to General You Know Who,
And ask him over here to reign as our King Roderick Dhu.

Radio Forth Poem 4

BLUE IS IN

When we were kids, we used to find the Public Library
A far less welcoming affair than what it is to-day;
I daresay we were bright-faced boys, with frank and earnest looks,
But nobody was going to let to let us loose among the books.

If we ever thought about it, no doubt we understood
There was no implication that we'd pinch them if we could;
That was the system then, and so we took it as we found it,
Although our literary tastes were apt to be confounded.

You found the number of your book by subject and by class
In battered leather catalogues with corners made of brass,
And then you had to find it in a whopping big glass case
With numbers either red or blue, each in its proper place.

If that should be your lucky day, your number would be blue;
You only had to ask for it, and it was brought to you.
But if you found that it was red, you had to go without,
For Blue was in, the notice said, and Red, alas! was Out.

But even if you got your book, you might be disenchanted
To find it wasn't quite the sort of thing you thought that you had wanted.
The title of a book might seem to promise lots of fun,
But when you got your hands on it, you found that you'd been done.

These better days, they let us in to see the books ourselves;
They open doors, and trust us with the freedom of the shelves;
They help us if we ask them, or else they let us be:
There's no place like a library, to let us feel we're free.

I know it's wrong to tolerate the sort of thief who baffles
Proprietors of locks and bolts, like that fictitious Raffles,
But I hate far more bitterly that sneaking sort of crook
Who takes this easy chance he's given now, and steals a book.

[To Sydney Tremayne] 28 Feb 75

...I look at *Calgacus* with suspicion, and indeed I am worried to
hear Marxist noises getting loud in the Scottish self-government
movement. There has long been a lot of talk about a workers'
republic etc from C. M. Grieve etc, but I thought it was too

ridiculous. Now, I begin to fear that nothing is ever so ridiculous as not to be worrying. Sorley Maclean has been communistically inclined for a long time, largely because, I think, of the unjust treatment of the people of Raasay especially. Big Mary of the Songs, I'm told, was cheated early in life and produced much angry poetry in consequence, so she may be caused to sing in the Exploitees' Chorus of our Holy Workers' Opera....Big Mary of the Songs, I understand, was a very fine poet, and so is Sorley Maclean, and he is a very good man, too, and possibly not very wary in the presence of the unscrupulous.

[To Alex Anderson]   7 March 75

...This *Open Space* is quite astonishingly good, especially, I thought, the story, "Jerusalem – Vienna," that is to say, among those by people whose work I didn't know already. That story shows accomplishment in many ways, and one that you don't notice till the end is that it goes round in a circle. I doubt if I have ever read a story so short that ranged so widely, and yet made a complete whole: this is an extraordinarily well-written piece.

In fact this applies, I think, to the whole magazine. That piece by A.A. – I'm so pleased to find a poet wrestling or warslin with Einstein, and in Scots, too, which we think of as a language that can express anything. And this poem is a joke, the only thing that can come out of this rum situation – a joke being the putting into its jocular place of a state of affairs that a practical person is not prepared to take seriously, no matter how logical or even real it may be. WHO is A. A., for Guidsake? This magazine just throws up these things by the way, it would seem. I like David Radd, too, anent his Girl from Inverurie (in the Geery land, if I'm not misinformed). I can't give all your items the full treatment, these are the bits I noticed most. I should like to send you something but have little to send, because I'm having too much fun, like Harriet. But here is a piece you may print if you wish.

P.S. ...ask A. A. to gloss *a cack haun.*

Note: the magazine in question was *Open Space* No. 2, published from Aberdeen University English Department, January 1975. The story referred to was by William Watson. And the poem Garioch sent was "Hysteria," which was printed in the next issue.

[To J. B. Caird]   15 March 75

I have just learned good news that my book is no deid yet, after all. I was out for a walk that included a free read of the papers in St. Whatsit's Apse in Chalmers Close (immortalised by the Chalmers press, which *nearly* rented a shed there) and so I was going home via Jeffrey Street and saw a shop window with books, and lukit in and lukit in, and keekit ben and keekit ben, and out came Dave Morgan, formerly employed by Southside, and askit me in. There I learned that Canongate Publishers (it's their premises) had bought up Southside, and were going to publish my book after all. I was pleased with these good tidings, not half!

[To Sydney Tremayne]   12 May 75

...Ah yes, I would have been no great shakes as a journalist, having nothing but a prose style....So I applied for the Teachers' Training College, so late that I hoped I wouldn't be admitted. I did in those days (1932-33) look with a speculative eye on those down-and-outs in the Grassmarket. I made an attempt to get a job on *The Edinburgh Evening Dispatch*, and in the final year at school I had tried to learn shorthand at the night-school. I could write it, so I fondly thought, but could not read it, except for Dear Sir, We are in receipt of your esteemed favour of...bits, most unlikely to help a chap to report a Moseley march or something like that. Ah well, it's a good job I got into teaching, rather unexpectedly. I suspected I had got in on somebody else's bribe, as throughout the interview the tableful of Education Committeemen kept calling me Mr Somebody-else, and I was too shy to contradict them. What luck! Well, it all happened for the best: here I sit in my slippers, while more deserving men splash about their business in the rain outside, and Thursday is OAP day. And Friday was Peneng Day (English teaching pension). And nine days before that was Penscot Day!...

[To Sydney Tremayne]   12 Dec 75

...Oh yes, The Royal High School—some years ago we were told in many speeches quoted by *The Scotsman* and *The Edinburgh Evening News* that its building was no longer suitable. We used to

E   65

think it was all right, except for a few odd things—the open coal fires did not send their heat to the back of the classrooms, especially when the teacher stood in front of the fire and spread out his gown to catch the radiance. The boys usually scramble for the back seats, but it was the opposite way round for us during most of the year. I remember one of those speeches made by a councillor who described it as a "slum school." It was a bit inconvenient because we had a lot of walking through the rain between classes, but that did not worry us. In fact, the corridors are quite cleverly arranged. Anyhow, they built an ordinary modern pile near the city boundary on the edge of a wood, now called The Royal High School but known to the staff familiarly as "Barnton Comprehensive." We as boys were much impressed by our splendid building, and there were wonderful places underneath it that we called The Dungeons, reached by going down steps and getting a hyste up through a hole in some railings and dreeping down inside, then down a steep slope, all stone, and through a wet passage on the left. It was on the side of the Calton Hill, and maybe that was drainage out of the rocks. It ought to be fine for The National Assembly. There is a fine hall. I don't know why they don't use the Old Parliament House, however. It is only used by lawyers, or advocates, rather. Apparently they walk up and down till someone comes along with a brief: the young ones get a lot of exercise....

[I've also] received about a forpit of books, no, nearer half a stone, of poetry and prose, partly in English but mostly in Italian. And I still feel the surprise I felt as a schoolboy when told that Dryden's satires and Milton's *Areopagitica* had caused such sensations, as I had looked at them and could not believe that anyone could ever read them at all. The same goes for those books for the writing of which so many religious people burned one another in the 16th and 17th centuries. I would like leave to be just stupid for a while, but these learned people come along with books, having apparently got the impression from me that I am one of themselves. I must be a remarkably good con-man.

[To Derek Bowman]   16 Feb 76

...Yes, please recommend my book [*Two Men and a Blanket*]; it all helps. I'm to read it on the B.B.C. in ten instalments of fifteen minutes each, what luck! I've just finished chopping it into sections of 2,300 words each. It is interesting to see how it may be compressed, but, given notice, I would rather read the whole thing, for no extra charge....

Producing plays, now, that must take a lot of doing, let alone in German. The whole atmosphere of the stage is strange to me, however.

Note: D. B. produced Georg Büchner's *Woyzeck* at the Adam House Theatre.

[To a Friend]   19 October 76

Sydney Tremayne's Gairloch is not your Loch Fyne Gareloch, so far as I can make out. I wonder if it does any good to cut bracken: probably yes, I should think, only there is not labour enough, not even schoolboys, I shouldn't wonder, nowadays. I do remember a little book published by enthusiastic people who had all sorts of ideas to do something worthwhile with the soil, if that's the right word for it, of the Highlands and Islands. I wrote an enthusiastic review of that book in *Scottish International Review* which some curmudgeonly fool described as more suitable for the *Farmers' Weekly*, as if that were a term of condemnation! Oh, 'ow fairylike can these lit-wits become? Anyhow, Sydney Tremayne is now established in his house called "Minchview" at Peterburn, Gairloch, Wester Ross. He seems to have arrived in a pretty Heilant situation, including Finley's "terrifying scraps of flex" which is his electricity supply from Sydney's house—"He works an electric cooker off this contraption."

[To J. B. and J. Caird]   20 Dec 76

...Callum Macdonald called my attention to a Tom Scott Double Bumper Number of *Scotia* that annoyed him, and no wonder, for in it T. Scott says that the *Selected Poems* of mine that Macdonald published was done at my own expense. Not, repeat not! Well, for one thing I have composed an epistle of well-chosen words which I shall post to Mr Morrison on 25 Dec., when goodwill to all mankind is due to be at its height. Morrison's weak editing really won't do. He disclaims responsibility for his contributors' views, but must surely be answerable for matters of fact, at least of this kind. I was affected by the experience of seeing that ancient kirk on the top of the hill on a bleak day. I shall remember that, and also I shall remember your very good fireside. Also I was glad to hear John Ogdon playing such miraculous pianistics. We had been wondering so much about him. I liked your theatre too. It does make our bosses look silly, but there seems to be no sign of that happening. . . .

Note: the kirk referred to was the ruined church of Barevan near Cawdor in Nairnshire.

[To Derek Bowman] 6 Jan 77

Here, for amusement only, is a copy of the Radio Forth piece, duly performed. (D.P. — I wonder if the University of Edinburgh still issues these faintly-praising damns: I collected a few of them in my day.) Well, anyway, I remembered that my new date of recording is Thurs. not Fri. so I duly wrote this Battery Hen piece, and I am much beholden to you for suggesting it. MORAL: I should go about more and meet people. I'm not sure, but my new slot may not involve or carry the irksome privilege of transmitting one of these per week into the empty Aether (and I at least for one don't know how empty it becomes when I draw back the curtain: I feel more strongly about this than one might perhaps expect, but only when I happen to be thinking about it; thinking and remembering and feeling strongly are all interconnected and indeed I practise niggardliness in matters of remembering, as in many other lines of behaviour.) I must say our room has got warmer in the last half hour, because of various causes, but mainly, I think, because thirty-five minutes ago I, hearing the wind making a noise about conveying my expensive warmth from point A to point B, sealed up the sash with tape and shut the shutters also. I really started off with intent to say I was sorry about your dog Tam, and to reflect upon the chains of coincidences that result in sadness or in narrow squeaks, like the time I was going too fast on my motor-bike to turn a sharp corner in the Heilands somewhere and had to drive straight at the bank, which in fact was not two feet high, but just a lot of long grass. It is only chance that determines these things, whatever the Romans may have believed.

THE BATTERY HEN SPEAKS

Don't you believe their clever arguments, when people say
I must enjoy this kind of life, or else I wouldn't lay,
Every two days, three eggs, instead of just the usual two,
Responding to electric dawns as I'm supposed to do.

Don't you believe them when they say my cage is just the size
For me, because I'm lazy and averse to exercise,
And that it's wide enough all round, and really rather high,
Since I'm not keen on walking, and would never want to fly.

Talking about flying, don't believe that, of all things
You associate with hens, the least important are our wings;
The expert likes to tell you we are growing them so small
That some day he may breed us without any wings at all.

It's uncommon civil of him, is it not? to keep in mind
Our welfare; don't you think that expert's really very kind;
I daresay you consider him a rather decent chap:
How convenient it would be for us to have no wings to flap!

Supposing I could move about, I'd maybe never try it.
Why should I? They provide me with a nicely-balanced diet
That never fails; here nothing ever happens unforeseen,
For everything is automatic, worked by a machine.

That expert's so efficient at conditioning us hens,
We suit his purposes in our neat rows of little pens;
Maybe his methods might be made to work with people, too:
Take a good look at me. He may be planning this for you!

[To a Friend]   12 January 77

I was typing this little piece to read tomorrow and put in a carbon
for you: it is just a bit of fun. There are only two left after this.
Radio Forth are cutting costs, and I'm one of them, but they are
letting me complete my century. It has taken two years, and I have
had a good innings. I've asked them to let me continue as their Poet
Laureate (I spell it without inverted commas) but honorary and
without duties. But if I feel like it and want to send out a poem
occasionally perhaps they will let me, for nothing. We didn't really
have any snow this morning, none to speak of; I only needed that
snow, for the sake of rhyme, but it has been freezing, sure enough.

Sydney Tremayne and his wife Connie...I visited them by good luck in November, and found them in a really good croft house, with the previous crofter not far off (he has kept the land and has a few sheep on it), with the sea (the Minch) just down the road, and down a cliff. It was terribly windy during the three days when I was there. The wind roared in the lums just like the noise of a jet aeroplane and the roof rattled. The slates are fixed with copper wires or something: ordinary fixings won't do for that place. It was a bit of luck that took me there: I was asked to do a reading at schools in Tain, Invergordon, Dingwall, Fortrose and Plockton. That is their usual plan: it is too far to invite somebody to only one school. That was a great experience. Peg and I had a trip on the Kyle line once in summer on an excursion, and we had been on that line from Inverness to Dingwall and Thurso, but we didn't stop, of course, except for a while at Kyle of Lochalsh. It was very different in winter. I got out at Achnasheen on the way back from Plockton, and Mr and Mrs Tremayne met the train with their van and trundled me to Peterburn where they live. On the following Monday they trundled me to Achnasheen again, quite a long way, and I came home by Inverness. It was quite an adventure....

I'm sorry to have been so long about writing: it is not right. I am getting almost uncontrollably lazy: Peg, on the other hand, has become very much interested in drawing and painting. She always could draw and paint, but now she is trying to learn perspective and generally to train herself, mostly out of books. This is very good, and she is quite fresh in a way that I am not. Well, I have been getting ready the copy and very carefully reading proofs for my *Collected Poems*, and become embarrassed at reading them so often, trying to eliminate misprints. I am unpleasantly conscious that there is not much new in this book, except for a lot of translations.

Radio Forth Poem 98

CHOP-CHOP!

I thought it might be fun if we should have a little look
At what I found this morning: it's a yellow-covered book
Called *Pidgin-English Sing-Song*, dated 1876;
Him blong one hundred years ago, him Pidgin-speakee tlicks.

It happened that we'd had a rather heavy fall of snow, down
Our way, so I went bottom-side our house, look-see our go-down
To catchee spade for my to clear chop-chop him snow away,
And there I found him Sing-Song Book, long time no see, hullay!

70

That book was meant for sailors and our business-men, out East,
So they could learn to make themselves half-understood, at least,
By China-boy him thinky no belongy smart inside,
So larn Chinee they no can do, allo fan-kwei topside.

In case you missed that bit, they found posh foreigners too dim
To learn enough Chinese to ask one question, make chin-chin;
Mo betta handsome talkee hab got China-boy, ph'ho!
(That's just an interjection) fan-kwei loosee face, galow!

Pidgin is only *business*, mispronounced, and so *joss-pidgin*,
Since *joss* is *deos*, Portuguese for *god*, must mean *religion*.
Even an Auld Kirk minister, believe it if you can,
Had to get used to being known as *him joss-pidgin-man*.

That's how it used to be, a hundred years ago, at least,
According to my yellow-covered Sing-Song Book, out East;
I daresay it's quite different now, in far Chan-chi-lee-hong
(I found that in the Glossary)—Chancery Lane, Hong-Kong.

[To Sydney Tremayne]   12 April 77

Here you are, this confident looking volume [*Collected Poems*,
Macdonald] soon to appear in the face of all likelihoods, entirely
thanks to M. Macdonald plus the Scottish Arts Council, but
especially plus Callum Macdonald's goodwill and, in fact,
patriotism. But I am inclined to regard this handsome volume as a
wreath. Awell, never mind: you will find here not much or anything
you have not seen before. "Macalaster" [see *Complete Poetical
Works*, p. 169]—that is a Lamsdorf [i.e. P.O.W.] piece so
generally thought not good that I even forgot about it: many people
I respected were much against it. . . .

[To a Friend]   16 April 77

I was pleased to get your letter, and it just happened the next day
or so some advance copies of the *Collected* arrived, and here is one
with my compliments, and I'm very pleased to have it to give to
you. There is not much here that has not been published before, I'm
afraid: it rather looks as if my original poetry is exhausted; well,
that does happen, I think, and even translation seems to need
unwilling effort, so the whole thing may as well have a rest. But this
is a well-produced book, and Callum Macdonald has put no end of
care into printing it. . . .

You do well to have so many Neil Gunn novels: they are said to be scarce. A friend of mine, J. B. Caird, knows a great deal about these novels, and has written about them. Also, he lives in Inverness, and I think Neil Gunn was in the Black Isle, and they would meet. In fact, he bought a very nice small picture which was not being much sought after at the displenishing sale. I don't know anything about its value, but it is good to have. I visited Caird on the way home from Gairloch (or rather, Peterburn) and noticed that picture. I haven't read many of those novels myself, and not *The Green Isle.*...I'm pretty cheerfully ill-read, in fact. Caird reads everything, and always has done. We marvelled at him away back in our student days. He has even written an article proving pretty conclusively by quotations that J. M. Barrie could have been a very good Scottish novelist if he had not gone after the big money....

[To J. B. Caird]   21 April 77

Your piece about J. M. Barrie seems to me just what the magazine [*Brunton's Miscellany*, edited by Morley Jamieson] needs: the point about Barrie (and J. Buchan) going for the big (English) money rather than writing as well as they might, seems to me well-proved by the very useful quotations. I don't know that anybody else would have had the conscientiousness to read Barrie thoroughly enough to find how good a writer he could have been, and what service he could have done for the Scottish novel, so it is a good job you took the trouble....

What you say shortly about J. Buchan made me fetch out two books that somehow are about, though I don't know how they got here. We have for many years kept *Memory Hold the Door* handy because it fits just right under the drawing-room door, which has funny hinges that make it shut of its own accord. But for once I read it, well, skimmed through it anyway, with some surprise, and did the same to *Unforgettable, Unforgotten* by his sister "O. Douglas" whose books were in our house when I was so-high. I was surprised how successful Buchan was in getting into places like the G.H.Q. and that sort of thing right away, and into Parliament for the Scottish Universities, nae bother, and into the Commissioner's gold-plated job, and that of the Governor-General, title and all.

Yes, he took sasine all right: I noticed that. And how nicely he became a partner in Nelson's! He also could write, sure enough. I can remember only a little about *Witch Wood*, which also I read when I was so-high, because it was about the house, but it fascinated me horribly, especially some kind of circular dance of witches, enjoyably obscene. I can even remember reading it in our front parlour, surreptitiously, I shouldn't wonder. But of course I forget what the story was about.

Of course he is writing about himself in *Memory*..., and not boasting, not being Cecil King, but you can't help seeing how he landed lucky so many times, and wondering at his confidence, and wishing for assurance of his ability at running improved concentration camps and publishing houses, and secret services, never mind an Assembly and a Dominion, and wondering how much of his getting-on was due to a narrative invention and a vigorous style.

I suggested to Morley a point that might be added to your Barrie piece, if you agree. Having gone for the money so long in such a big way, there he was in the Adelphi, in the finest residential quarters in London, with a drawerful of cheques he was too apathetic to put through the bank. Is this story true, I wonder? I have no idea where I learned it. But it might well be added to give a sense of futility.

[To a Friend]   1 June 77

Having got this book out [*Collected Poems*] I can't stand the idea of writing poetry, or even of translating Belli, meantime, but an interesting thing happened last week when a magazine called *The New Review* sent me a book to review which is largely taken up with Belli and with the translation of his sonnets. This makes me feel like Red Adair. I sent off that review and hope it has arrived in time.... Even the writing of plain English worries me, as you can see by the corrections, but that may be due to a strange job I have been doing for M. Macdonald, the publisher to whom I am so much beholden. It is a History of the Clan Donald that he is publishing. It is a most interesting book, but written in a style of English that goes wrong rather often, and gets the words into a queer order, as I with difficulty do not do now, or try at least, so I have been tidying it up as well as I can. Apparently one difficulty is

73

that its grammar is often that of Gaelic; also it is largely taken from the records of shennachies (if that is the right spelling) with old-fashioned punctuation that may have been added later, I don't know. Anyhow, I shall have to read much Daniel Defoe before I get my own style into any decent order again.

[To Sydney Tremayne] 15 Aug 77

That poem of S. Maclean is comical, right enough, or ridiculous at least, "The Nightmare," I mean. It would be dreadfully serious to him. I don't know what all that trouble was about Eimhir, and would be too embarrassed to ask....But as for his adjectival elaborations (inflations) I always just suppose that the Celts write like that and it would go very well in Gaelic. But every word in your letter (about his Marxist religiosity and want of even ordinary clear observation of ordinary things as they are) is bang on target.... Caird thought MacDiarmid had been pushed during all these years into stupid attitudes by crowds of stupid admirers, or, what is worse, by unscrupulous operators who wanted to use him. And indeed I think of him as a woolly lamb, and Sam Maclean also, intelligent all right, but so soft emotionally that they give up thinking when their feelings take over. And it is a damned disgrace how the political hard men will take advantage of decent people who are genuinely upset when they see people being badly treated. All the same, I don't know how intelligent people can be made to respond, without thinking, to meaningless emotive words, like squaddies on their square-bashing. That really beats me. And how can a poet, with words and images and puns as his stock-in-trade, be apparently carried out of his wits by a Russian pun? And then this poet extends his pun to a metaphor, and becomes a poet of a red Scotland, especially a poet who likes to go out and paint the town red of a Saturday and feels pretty blue on the Sunday and hates the church bells because he has such a headache....

I remember how shattered Sam Maclean was when Russia signed the non-aggression pact, and also how apologetic when the Red Army showed up not very well in Finland. But why? Because Russia was the Promised Land, or rather the Land of Heart's Desire; of course the P.L. was full of Caananites, full of ideological error. It really is a serious matter, and I am vexed that

Grieve should not have honestly and seriously considered what his preaching had to do with real life, which he should have known something about, as a journalist, even in Montrose....

[To a Friend] 28 October 77

On Wednesday evening we opened [your] Glenfiddich. Peg is 99.9% teetotaler, but she had a cold and was becoming glum, so I offered her a glass with a lot of boiling water and a little of The Mercies and I had some too, the other way round. Peg has been making a big sketch of a corner at Stockbridge, for her next painting; it does really look good, and what's more, I listened eagerly to what she had to say, which doesn't always happen. She works on these plans or sketches or pictures in her head, telling me all about them, and mostly I'm not much help, though she does like me to listen, and is very keen to be advised (she is not at all sure of herself as a painter, etc., and is far better than she thinks, or so it seems to me) only I don't know anything about it, but can only offer ignorant well-meant comments. Well, we had one or two more doses of what the doctor ordered, and I cannot speak too highly of the beneficient effects of that splendid present. And, having paid attention to what Peg had to say, I read her this new sad poem, the first I have managed to write for a long time, "The Maple and the Pine" [*Complete Poetical Works* p. 208], which therefore made me happy to have finished it, that afternoon, and she did agree that it is a good one, though very sad, certainly, more so in the end perhaps than it needed to be, because I couldn't resist the allusion to MacPherson in "MacPherson's Farewell." They have the remains of that fiddle (MacPherson's) somewhere in a museum (the one he broke). I have seen a photo, which looks as if the fiddle is not beyond repair, using the instructions in my father's book, but I daursay the Heilanmen wad regaird me in the licht of wan that wid pit back the airms on the Venus de Milo....

[To Joyce Herbert] 17 March 78

...the word *shouglie*. This bothered me a good deal, because it has come to be a comic word through its associations; in fact, the Scots language has been so much used on the stage by comedians (some very good (Tommy Lorne) and some a bad influence (Harry Lauder), only that is too long a story for now), so it is easier to use Scots for comic than for serious purposes. But I thought it worth while to give a shouglie or shooglie a chance, and used it for the Red Sea! Indeed it might make you laugh if you saw the cliff of water shaking above you, even if it was a very nervous kind of laugh. All this may not help the language much, but it is just as well to have a try. The nobill toun doesn't smell of haddocks etc., though I always think about a square mile of Aberdeen smells of fresh fish, but Edinburgh smells of malt being boiled with hops. They have built a giant brewery just west of centre, so much for our being east-windy, west-endy, only that was always wrong, for our prevailing wind is west, just as everywhere else in this country, so our posh streets are on the west side, just as usual, more or less. Anyway, when the wind is west, the whole town smells of malt and hops, and for my part I think that is all right.

I'd better explain that the introduction to Jephthah etc is in large part put into Scots from a letter I had from George Davie, which was so informative and so well-expressed that it only needed a straightforward translation to go into that rigorously Scots book (overdone, I daresay) where there is no glossary, and even *copyright* becomes *copyricht*.

A thought occurs to me. They do sometimes, though with decreasing frequency. I shall enclose a dust-cover. I had these made recently, so as to sell some copies, of which I have many stacked between the ceiling of our hall and the upstairs floor, and Dave Morgan, who travels for Canongate, has decently agreed to sell them for me, and is succeeding. I have long thought that J. and B. needed an energetic salesman. And a dust-cover. So here it is.

[To J. B. Caird]   21 Dec 78

(This is mostly about these obsequious obsequies on Hugh MacDiarmid in *Lines*.)

I have been looking at *Lines* 67, at the articles on Hugh MacDiarmid's poetry and his influence, etc., and wonder much and also should like to know what you think. R. Watson (p. 15 ff), of whom I think highly, takes the lines:

> Wunds wi warlds to swing
> Dinna sing sae sweet,
> The light that bends owre a'thing
> Is less ta'en up wi't.

He finds an ambiguity: (a)(i) "the bereaved mother sings more sweetly than the winds that move the worlds," and (a)(ii) "she is enveloped in her grief more completely than even the rays which curve through space and envelop us all." (b)(i) "the cosmic winds do not sing so sweetly as a lass wi tousie hair," and (b)(ii) "the light that bends over everything is not involved with her and her loss."

Now I see no difference between (a)(i) and (a)(ii). And (b)(i) seems the same as (b)(ii) once I have sorted out the phraseology of the critic.

I think Watson is thinking that the licht is less concerned with a'thing than the lass is concerned with the bairn, and also less concerned with a'thing. But I do think he is making an ado over naething much. Then he makes a technical point (p. 16, 1.9) of the "curiously curt, elided, words" etc ("ta'en" and "wi't"). But these are the ordinary Scots words used by H. MacD. and nearly everybody else who uses Scots in any context.

Note also 4 lines quoted top p. 17:

> "Ah!" you say, "if only one of these stones would move
> — Were it only an inch — of its own accord
>   This is the resurrection we await,
> — The stone rolled away from the tomb of the Lord."

Now, I ask, what reader, here familiarly addressed as "you," would ask that? Not any Christian, certainly, for he would know that the stone rolled away long ago, but only because the Lord pushed it.

Then H. MacD. addresses us as "detached intellectuals" (by what right, I ask; does he know who his readers are?) and this leads to:

> — I lift a stone; it is the meaning of life I clasp
>   Which is death, for that is the meaning of death;

Now I think that is a useless statement, whether it is taken literally or figuratively. And if it is meant to have practical truth, then I am seriously doubtful if that sort of idea of practical truth is worth considering. (I admit I have introduced that idea myself, so maybe nobody would have suggested that nonsense anyway. I was only trying to be helpful.)

I do think a critic, who can so keenly see an ambiguity that is only a way of saying the same thing twice, should look very hard at "—I lift a stone...meaning of death." He should look hard at the word *meaning* and tell us what it means in this context.

A critic here should be very wary, to avert the danger of my suspecting that H. MacD.'s profundity here is that of a well which looks "wondrous deep" because it is "wondrous dark," though it is really shallow, and contains only "a little dryness and dirt."

To revert to the quote from "Empty Vessel," I would take that as a simple and sad and moving poem. No critical subtlety required. And it is "wondrous deep." (If we don't enquire too closely into "cosmic winds.")...

On p. 15 of *Lines* Mr Murison, an undoubted *savant*, ends his article, having said some sensible things by the way, with this paragraph:

> MacDiarmid led a Scotland which had lost its way after 1918 on to a certain and defined path, which requires mental effort and moral courage, the only one which for that reason has a future. After MacDiarmid, as after Knox, Scotland will never be the same place again.

I daresay it will be *in* the same place, but let that pass. I suspect that Murison just could not bear to leave out the word *place*, being vaguely half-aware that he was using that wearisome phrase once more again. How could it be the same as it was in 1918?

BUT seriously, what was that path? It was supposed to lead to a Scottish workers' (atheist, no doubt) republic à la John Maclean. Not everybody's republic, notice. The Kulaks would have to be liquidated, for one thing. The path also led to a mixture of things. I think everybody was to write (speak?) Scots, or everybody was to write (speak?) Gaelic, etc., etc. I suppose every poet would have to write the kind of poetry MacD. wanted. What's all this about mental effort and moral courage? Of course there's not much future otherwise. Does Father Anthony Ross, whom I happen to think of, try to get along without m.e. and m.c.? And what path is he on? And what about the S.N.P.? On p. 14 Murison gets all taiglit with MacD.'s *splairging* (the word used by Archie's father in *Weir of H.*) more or less deciding that it is O.K. for great poets to splairge, unless I am unfair to him, which I think not.

Even Daiches waffles, with this sort of statement: "Self-contradiction is for MacD. a mode of poetic awareness." Awareness? Surely not! Was he cognizant of observed objects as both bandy-legged and knock-knee'd simultaneously? (Or is *poetic* an all-purpose let-out word?) And of course the fallacious thought that this, like a lot of other things, is peculiarly Scottish. Whereas D. H. Lawrence admired Walt Whitman for saying "Very well, I contradict myself. I am infinite. I contain multitudes." A poor argument, I have always thought. He was not infinite, and multitudes are not the same as infinity; but it is boring to destroy self-evident fallacies. I suppose that would be the Mid-Atlantic Antisyzygy!

All these futile efforts of able Scottish critics, maybe show why as the egregious (and rightly so, I daresay: he sent a mighty fine Christmas card, "Coronation of the Virgin" (sad reminder of coronary thrombosis and paralytic strokes) from a French Book of Hours c. 1500 (Edinburgh University Library MS 43) addressed to "Mr and Mrs Robert G Sutherland" postmarked 12 December. It was nice of him, and of course he wouldn't know, and all well-meant. I am methodically marking all Christmas cards addressed to "Mr and Mrs Sutherland" with the note "M & M", meaning to write later to all the people who sent them.) (That was a big parenthesis, and sure to happen.) To continue from just before the opening bracket above (the egregious) Robert Preston Wells, contributing his article (p. 9) on "MacDiarmid and America" can only give detailed information on how MacD. has not been heard of in the U.S.A.

Yes, that big parenthesis was bound to come: I wake up with thoughts of Peg, and so it is nearly all day. I hope it is not going to go on too long like this.

Yours sincerely,
Robert G. Sutherland
without remede.

PS: To sum up: it seems that in poetry one is not expected (by Scots obsequious critics) to write sense (provided that one is a Great Man).

...Mr and Mrs Miller are coming, I think, in the third week of January, and they can have Room 4 on B Deck (the upstairs counts as A Deck, and Matthew Moulton is happy in the Steerage) though they will have to look after themselves mostly. They live in Gloucester (in a house called Rivendell) and we met them because when we lived in Hayes our Helen and their daughter were in the same class at Bromley Grammar School. He has since become famous as a (or nowadays *the*) translator of Hegel. He first learned German as a P.O.W. in the 1914-18 War. He gave me two books by Hegel, *Philosophy of Mind*, translated by William Wallace, with the *Zusätze* (extra bits by Hegel's students, I think these are) translated by A. V. Miller, and also *Logic*, translated by William Wallace. I believe Mr Miller is most famous for his translation of Hegel's *Phenomenology*, which he did not give me, wisely, perhaps, because it is said to be very difficult, and I cannot make anything of any one page of the other books (an exaggeration? Only a small one, if that). Mr Miller translated this all by himself, and the philosophers regard it as the standard English translation for a long time to come, most likely. Wallace is quoted as writing: "The *Phenomenology of Spirit* of 1807 was the flight of a young Pegasus on which only a kingly soul could soar to the empyrean of the Idea; it might have all the 'diamond purity' of Hegelianism, but only consummate skill and patience could hope to use it with advantage." So, you see, what chance have I got?

I don't know how it is, but I can't stand poetry, though I do try. It became 8.30 four minutes ago, and I turned on Poetry Now on the wireless, as planned, and had to switch it off, though there was nothing wrong with the programme. What makes this worse is that I got a letter early in October offering me a whole 20 minutes to myself on Radio 3, from an agreeable man in Manchester, Fraser Steel, whom I met in May at a poetry affair in Leeds in which I took part and enjoyed myself. I said yes but couldn't come to Manchester because Peg was ill (I thought at that time she would get better) and he said he would come to Edinburgh, but things got worse and I said I would send a script early in the New Year and now of course I could go to Manchester, but not in this weather (I hope it will be clear by the 12th) but so far I just can't, though it only involved picking out some suitable poems and doing a bit of intro. and linking and seeing about the timing, and I can't.

For a while I couldn't even sleep at night recently, a bad business, followed by a spoilt day, and not one at a time either, but I have cured that by reading as my book at bedtime Hegel's *Philosophy of Mind*, complete with Mr Miller's translation of the Extra Bits.

In fact, though there are a good many books in the house, there is great difficulty in finding any to read. Luckily I tried Hugh Miller's *My Schools and Schoolmasters* once more, with very good results of pleasure and profit. It is well-written, and especially it has a manly cheerfulness, and bears no grudge. By comparison, I conspue (*sic*) e.g. L. G. Gibbon, and *The House with the Green Shutters*, and H. G. Wells' *Tono Bungay* (I nearly wrote *Tono Pandy*), which I fetched out in desperation, which is full of grudges and sneers. I don't just hate those "bodies" of Gibbon and the other fellow whose name I forget. I hate their books.

This afternoon there was a slight thaw, and I went out to the nearest reasonably cheap supermarket (Templeton's in Leith Street, in that horrible new building) wearing my army boots and army greatcoat and the bottoms of my trousers rolled, and I daresay it was hardly panic-buying, but I fetched my basket home just about as heavy as I could carry.

PS These letters don't need answering. You are liable to get a lot of them, as things now are.

[To J. B. and J. Caird]   31 Jan 79

...I very much enjoyed visiting George Davie and Elspeth yesterday. What a lot he knows, and she also, and how pleasant it was to listen and to talk! (I read (present tense) things out rather loudly to myself for fear I might have to do a reading in a hall, with no voice, for lack of using it.) (I daresay Peg and I used to talk a lot without realising it, or a good deal, at any rate.) George Davie had read the *Chapman*, and agreed that you made a much better job of your piece (a difficult job, certainly) than the other three, which is an understatement by a mile, keeping it firmly in mind that yours is a funeral oration as well as the others, but it keeps to reason and good sense. Later, perhaps, a good critical work, much needed, will form a Part II. I cannot help thinking that it is not good that e.g. T. Scott should talk of him [MacDiarmid] in terms of Jesus Christ, and if MacD. asked for it in that unlucky triolet, misled by the

F   81

temptation of rhyme, I daresay: assume, doom, tomb, a man of sense who wished to praise him would keep that nonsense out of his obsequy.

Yes, with regard to Hegel, it seems that Karl Marx must have been no slouch to understand Hegel enough for Hegel to influence Marxism. But Hegel also influenced Hitlerism and Mussoism, did he not? How clever were these two, eh? I always wonder how these things happen. Could Marx, Hitler and Musso not think up their own devilry?

I wish I had not talked such a lot during that long visit to Davie's; I should have taken the chance when it came, and listened. A better idea would be to talk at home. All solitary people talk to themselves, all right, but I talk to Peg, which is an *eerie, eery* (I don't think I have ever written that word before) tendency I try to stop. How do you spell *eerie*, for goodness sake? It's not in Chambers Etymological English Dictionary. Not in Roget's Thesaurus. And it's not *eary*. Yes, it's in Collins Graphic English Dictionary (both *eerie* and *eery*), which my father won in 1905 as a First Prize for attendance at the Fountainbridge P.S.A. Brotherhood. Good, eh! Good practical sense. It is my principal dictionary, and has been, since I learned to read. And, by the way, it is nothing much to say of a poet that his work is deep, because the reader has to look up so many of his words in the Crossword Puzzlers' Dictionary, if he thinks it worthwhile, which it is to a Crossword Puzzler, I daresay.

But I am jaded, I know that, and would do well to avoid all reading of and about modern poetry. I have been getting on better with the *Lyrical Ballads*.

[To J. B. Caird]   10 March 79

...I got a copy of a book you recommended: *Zazie dans le Métro*, out of the public library. What a wealth of language! A lot of it, I regret, is not in my Petit Larousse. I did like, on almost the first page: "J'suis Gabriel, ton tonton." I lent it to Gerald, who knows French better than I, and he has been reading it with similar enjoyment and frustration. He even started to make a list of words, hoping to look them up in a Dictionary of Argot, if he could find one, but he gave up; there were too many. But we were both delighted with the Blondjinnezes. I thought it was a mistake in this fantastic book to spoil the fun by killing the widow, but others may think differently. I shall try to get *Le Vol d'Icare*. And à pro pro, I have been reading the A.S.L.S. postmortem tribute to Hugh MacDiarmid, which leaves me wondering how to distinguish between a colleur and a voleur.

[To J. B. Caird]   21 April 79

Tom MacDonald's book is out this week: *The Ministers*, published by the Souvenir Press, by grace of The Arts Council, under God, who comes into the story a good deal, at least by implication or by annexation. It is an unusual book, with quite a lot of bright description and vigorous incident on the way, and made out of a very short story, of great importance, however. Characters extremely good, all different, each consistent, minute in detail, convincing, I shouldn't wonder, certainly so to me, incapable as I am of surprise where the West Highlands are concerned (such is my ignorance) and sympathy-arousing. The style, I think, is a bit over-worked in the beginning, rather over-demanding attention mainly because of parenthetical clauses, but it clears as time goes on, like home-brew. It is certainly a notable book, and should have been published long ago, instead of being judged by the standards of ordinary novels. The idea of the whole thing is a real winner, and is well used; e.g. one of the ministers has a friend who saw some holy man in a church in Italy, where visions are so *O.K.* that a cleaner was irritated by having his attention called to such an ordinary occurrence as that holy man's feet firmly planted a couple of feet above the floor. Well done, Mary MacDonald, who survived all sorts of setbacks in trying to get it published.

I am now at my third Queneau: *Un Rude Hiver*. All three are very different. This one serious, realistic, with not many words that are in Petit Larousse. (Gerald took *Zazie* to read in Leith Reference Library, where they have Harrap's Dictionary of Argot, and found it very illuminating, full of connerie, but not at all emmerdant.) The Central Library also has *Le Vol d'Icare* and no more. I looked up *Vol* to find its gender. A very strange word, theft and flight, and *volage* = fickle (I thought it = theft), *volaille* I knew was poultry, odd, because they are not noted for their powers of levitation, though *volable*, I admit. Then *volant*, what a word! = shuttlecock, flounce, frill (my mother used to have what she called a "valance" round the beds to hide the kists stored underneath), an emmerdant arrangement: one bed was even raised for the purpose on four supports. We still have these things in the cellar somewhere. Was this a usual custom? Could you then buy these supports in any suitable shop? Could I sell mine for a lot of money to some imbécile?

I have more than ½ a mind to go to Paris for a week, pourquoi-pas? Make the foin while the £ shines. But even if the £ is high, so, they say, are French prices, même for the French. I don't care....

The coin that I find myself in is that even Garioch has become emmerdant (to me, at least). But Sutherland, my after all best friend, has cleaned up the windows and polished up the handle of the big front door.

PS: I guess that Queneau's *pissenlits* are dandelions. We called them peethebeds, during our later infancy, in our street.

[To Sydney Tremayne]   17 Jan 80

...I have always been interested in F. G. Scott, wondering why I never heard a performance of his songs. Long ago I tried to interest my cousin Johnnie Mathewson, baritone, who was a good singer, especially at Scots songs, telling him I would learn the piano accompaniments, but he did not respond....I once asked a well-known Scots singer at the Saltire Society, just the person likely to sing his songs, and she said singers didn't take to his songs because of his "ungrateful" vocal line—i.e. they were so unpleasant to sing. Now, H. MacDiarmid uttered one of his pulpit objurgations, for which he was so famous, and which he so much enjoyed objurgifying: "He never compromised in the slightest degree. Now in a country that is so utterly venal as Scotland, that was a priceless contribution. He was a pure artist and Scotland hasn't had many of them—in any connection at all." (I copied that from *The Radio Times*—of course they would quote that bit.) Interesting stress on the purity of the artist. He will not compromise. He knows best, or has access to heavenly guidance....Whereas Beethoven, a pianist, asked the advice of the violinist who was going to perform the violin concerto. Scott, a pianist, seemingly would not ask a singer if his voice-parts were singable. It looks like that. Why keep within a singer's compass anyway? A pure composer would not be compromised by anything so vulgar as vocal cords. This contemptuous word *venal* would cover this willingness to sell songs that singers can sing. (Also, I found the piano parts very difficult. But certainly Ronald Stevenson can manage them all right, so my inability doesn't matter.) All the same, does the non-venal artist never make things approachable by any but the Top People? Funny how communists should be like this! Ach well, I waste my time considering this absurd taking of things to their logical conclusions. Best to pay no attention to these rarified people and leave them to objurgate *in vacuo*.

[To J. B. Caird]   16 Feb 80

...I saw this afternoon by chance on the television an Open University aerial tour of Greece, which from the air looks a horrible country. Just when I came in they were showing how Sparta set about solving their overpopulation problem by getting very warlike and fighting their way over a range of 8,000 ft mountains (which they showed us and which make the Scottish Renaissance look overweening) into the next country (I forget its name) and after a lot of trouble turned its inhabitants into slaves or into rent-paying (50% of produce) farmers. (It would solve their population problem too.) They also turned their attention north to Arcadia (which I always thought was where good nature lovers went) but found it too barren to be worth while. Also we saw one pillar in Corinth, all that is left of Aphrodite's temple, to which the middle-distance runner Xenophon dedicated "ane hunder vicars," and the Parthenon at Athens which surprised me by looking in better repair in the middle section than is suggested by that very big model in some museum in London, I forget which.

I have since the New Year read much by and about Edwin (and Willa) Muir, having to talk about Edwin Muir on Tuesday at the Chaplaincy Centre. (But I've told them I can't go, because of this swollen face.) What happened was unexpected and simple. I met the Chaplain (a good and agreeable man I had met before, who stays round the corner, in Abercromby Place) in a pub I don't like all that much, as it is a bit lah-di-dah, called Leery the

Lamplighter's (it used to be the hairdresser's — corner of Picardy Pl and Dublin St) but it is the last before getting home and open till 11, I think (the Nelson is really the last, right opposite my house, but I don't go there (much) because it is dear, though I did go over there one day recently with Iain Crichton Smith, who stays there sometimes and rings my bell. . . .) Well anyway, I went into the Lamplighter place for just one pint, being full of beer and grief, each being partly the cause of the other, and the Chaplain came over to me with one more pint, really too many, and he persuaded me to promise this talk on Edwin Muir (my choice, I think) but I hadn't realised it was to be one of a series of high-powered talks and I was dismayed later to get the syllabus: a series of re-appraisals (how can I re-appraise E. Muir, after appraisal by Butter & Co?). I can't give this sort of lecture. I don't know enough. There were to be re-appraisals every Tuesday, a re-appraisal (that word looks queerer every time I write it). I have just looked up the syllabus. It is "re-assessment" — an even more alarming word for the reassessor. (There has been recently, or a few years ago, a re-assessment of this house, to my disadvantage.). . .

I broke off to watch "Thoroughly Modern Milly." Thoroughly enjoyed it.

PS: *Scott and Scotland* interested me. I was going to tell that meeting that the Scots Renaissance was a nuisance.

[To a Friend]   12 April 80

I have been obsessed with making a selection from Sir David Lindsay for the Carcanet Press people (Manchester), who have been good friends to me, and I really mean obsessed, I mean "persistently assaulted, especially by an evil spirit." Well, Lindsay is not that: he means only to make things better when times were very bad, but if you try to make a popular selection as this is meant to be, one of a series of early Scottish poets (Carcanet are doing good work for Scot. Lit.) you come up against non-literary problems of making cuts in his long works (he didn't write short pieces) and then his spelling has to be modernised slightly, but not spoiled, just so as to make it easy to read (he and his printers are haphazard especially about u, v, and w, so a simple word may look very strange) and my trouble is that I keep changing my mind and having to type pages all over (ower, ouer) agayn. Also the arithmetic is awkward, at least to me, but I solved that in the end by being careful about putting the paper into the typewriter so as to have 27 lines of average 10 words, knowing how that will fit into the printed page. I'm sorry to weary you with all this, but it is still rattling about in my mind though I posted the copy on Monday. And now I'm having a holiday.

[To Alistair Elliot]   18 June 80

I did not write "Lines on the Jordan," but would be proud to have done so. It is a splendid piece, with a dignified and resonant opening stanza, well-sustained, through a manly statement of intent justified from Holy Writ, to its conclusion giving generous advice to all. I like the way the kings are made one with the commoners, the lyrical second stanza, the words *fell* and *piddlin'*, pregnant with meaning, in the third and fourth, and likewise the associations of *tuneful prayers*. I am greatly obliged to you for placing in my hands a copy of this noble and witty work, especially as it was quite unknown to me. And I don't think it is in Wavell's *Poems from the Forces*. It is not included in *The Cruel Wars*, compiled by Karl Dallas (Wolfe Publishing Ltd., 10 Earlham Street, London WC2), which even has my "Kreigy Ballad," and I don't think it is in Hamish Henderson's *Ballads of World War II*, which I can't find, and wonder why; it is the sort of thing I may have lent to somebody. I shall take "Lines on the Jordan" in my pocket, and if I meet Hamish Henderson, as I often do, shall show it to him. "The Desert Lily" is also unknown to me, though it must be a notable poem.

PS's:
—Some of our blokes used to construct elaborate personal latrines on the sand, which were often completed just before we got orders to move.
—Hamish Henderson lately wrote a poem of which I think I remember a bit:

              have a look
To see what cruel war had done to bonnie Tobruk.
—I'm impressed by Colonel Gitaffy's wish to charge us rent for the

use of his desert. But he should be referred to the Eyeties. They did it first.

Note: The poem in question here was printed at the Eagle Press, Newcastle Library, in 1971, with the following note from Alistair Elliot:

"This 'Burns' poem was collected in the 15th Scottish General Hospital in Egypt about 1943 with another about the Desert Lily, a field lavatory with folding flower-like leaves. I would be interested to know more."

LINES ON THE JORDAN

In poes o' gold great kings mak' watter,
An' poorer folk in wooden platter.
Mony as 'twere a shameful matter
   Dae't withoot grace,
Like soakit souters aff a batter,
   Jist ony place.

Let me, in neuks where laden bees
Lilt love sangs tae the simmer breeze,
A blether fou, a mind at ease,
   Free o' a' chairge,
Shak' loose ma member as I please
   An' pish at lairge.

E'en sae did Adam, ere he fell
Tae secret piddlin'; Eve hersel'
Stroned guileless in a flowery dell
   Beside her jo —
Till Sawtan wi' a leer frae hell
   Brocht them a poe.

Wad ye seek Paradise,
Ye piddlin' mortals? Gin ye're wise
Shun platters, poes, an' a' sic vice:
   Seek Nature fair,
An' while yer tuneful prayers uprise
   Pish blissfu' there.

[To Alastair Mackie]   12 Sept 80

Thank you. That is a specially fine sonnet I hadn't found before. Not surprising: it is No. 1981. Maybe it should be done in Buchan speech, because your title "3 Louns and 9 Quines" is just right. Also it may be a help, because *quine* rhymes with *nine*. Maybe we should make it a joint effort, my Buchan being shaky? If I have a go, and manage to get the thing into shape, you might be so good as to do the finishing touches?

I'm tempted to use the once overworked word I came to dislike so much —*fizzen*. The temptation is that it rhymes with *prison*. Not a good idea? —maybe not. We'll see, I hope, if all goes well.

This is just a quick note. I have other fish to fry (breaded whiting frozen in Peterhead, 58p per pound) and it is now 12.35, dinnertime.

Note: Alastair Mackie's version of Belli No. 1981, "Three louns and nine quines" is as follows:

> Bairns? She'd a dizzen I'll tak my aith.
> Still she got them aa settled in.
> Gibbie and Eleck took to the claith.
> Angus? Weel, he's a jyle bird in Saughton.
>
> Lullie deid last year, and Sarah faith,
> she upped and awa wi a pinter loun.
> Jean's a kitchie-deem to abbots, sure's death,
> ye'd say they kiss the very hem o her goun.
>
> Mina's a hoose-keeper; Bridie's a weet nurse
> to an English body. Mallie, she took up wi, oh,
> a wastrel. Mina's a braw seamstress
>
> steeks in gowd. The last twa, Terry and Cleo,
> they werena pit to ony kinna trade,
> but still, they aye had a bob or twa they made.

[To Alastair Mackie]   27 Sept 80

Good, now we have two good translations, and if I publish mine I shall tell about yours, and maybe you will do the same for mine. They wouldn't combine; that was just a notion I had. Maybe I should have as title: "Three Laddies and Nine Lassies." That was a good idea: "aith — claith — faith — with." And "wi, oh — Cleo." Maybe *Cleo* could be put in line 13, and *job* in 12. Translating sonnets is a sair fecht, is't no? But fun. I wonder if the last line could have *still. Kitchie deem* is a first-rate word. I hadn't thought of it, and couldn't, in fact. I wonder how you seem to have room to spare in each line (apart from the last) — I have awful difficulties: Belli's language seems to take up less room than mine. . . .

The newspaper I use as a tablecloth has news that a chunk of stone fell off St. Giles' alleged cathedral, 80 ft. down to the main entrance. It is remarked as something surprising that it is not the 500-years-old crown that did it, but the 150-years-old restoration. That was a bad bit of work I have always regretted. They destroyed a wonderful Norman arch. They would have rebuilt the tower too, only funds fortunately gave out. And only think how many rascals might have been felled by that chunk of sandstone, if better directed! Including me? Cancel that thought.

[To Alastair Mackie]   5 Oct 80

The first thing I noticed about your new book is that you can write good poetry about a universal family grief, a thing I cannot do at all. I mean especially "The Day-Book o a Death," a very good poem, and quite long, and very well sustained, with each section complete in itself, and the sections varied and all fitting together. It is certainly one of the great subjects, for anybody who can use it, with all these regulation things that have to be done, just when grief is nearly out of hand: I remember especially going into an office where two red-faced enthusiastic sportsmen who looked like ex-cabbies were busy phoning to a bookie, and seeing them enter on duty in the crematorium, doing everything properly, and how their appearance in that office somehow cheered me up a bit. And there are the documents demanding information that you never thought of knowing, and all the rest of it. I have heard that in very cold countries they dig a number of graves estimated to be enough for the winter, before the frosts set in that will make digging impossible. More seemly than fetching in pneumatic drills, anyway. You make a good job of Orpheus, also, another thing very hard to do, or so I always thought, reading Sydney Smith's poem, and marvelling how good it is. But there is a lot of good poetry here, confident and reassuring. I am as sure as can be that someone always appears, and always will, who will keep the Scots poetry going strong like this.

PS: — I like your Thirties series very much. In Bellevue Road in the Twenties, no, earlier than that, even, we had a variant of "Eetle ottle black bottle" — "Eelie Olie dug's tolie" (or toalie?) which we considered very daring.

— Another grim memory: my father's funeral, very cold weather, Peg and I had meant to meet the cortege (what a word!) at Croydon, going there from home in Hayes in our motor-car. The lock of the car was frozen, the windscreen coated with solid ice. It's a long way by bus. We were not late, but it was so cold we did not stand at the gate, and did not meet properly. But we were finished in time for the next comer.

[To Alastair Mackie]   12 Oct 80

Yes, I should like very much to review your book if an editor asks me, and I hope one of them will.. . .

There is something to be said for having a book consistent throughout, either serious or less so. Ideally from this point of view one should have two books published about the same time, but it is hard enough to have one. And somehow one needs to publish some books, no matter how many poems may appear in periodicals. There was little notice taken of my poetry till Callum Macdonald published the *Selected*, and that might not have come out if Sydney Smith had not so persistently tried to have it done. Sydney could be practical and business-like: not everyone knows that.. . .

Right enough, *Hamewith's* popularity is a bit out of proportion, but not at the expense of other books, I'm sure. I look more and more doubtfully at the line of thought that thinks Scottish writing was all-bad until the advent of Hugh MacDiarmid, the All-good, and that such virtues as any of us now have are attributable to his redemption of us, and that we must therefore be always in danger of backsliding. A silly statement with a rhyme / May pass for Holy Writ through time. . .cf. "A Scottish poet maun assume etc." All the same, it is tiresome that so many people like Rock and Roll, but it can't be helped, and in fact doesn't matter, and its profits, they say, make it possible for recording companies to put out a lot of legitimate music.. . .

[To Alastair Mackie]   27 Oct 80

Carl MacDougall asked me to review *Back-Green Odyssey* for his magazine *Words*, and I have it half-done. It is a very good book, and I have been trying to explain what makes me think so.

PS — Please tell me sometime if the Skellies at Anstruther, or their name, I mean, is a variant of *skerries*. I once suggested that to Mr. Murison and he showed impatience. Maybe there is no recognised consonant change from *r* to *l*; I don't know. Jamieson gives *skerries* as rocks covered at high tide, and *skellyis* as rugged rocks (Douglas — Douglas was a Lothian man, I think. Maybe wrong). I expect there is no mystery about it. Haven't looked it up in S.N.D. Must do so, at the Library (can't afford £300) and see what Murison says.

Note: Garioch's review of *Back-Green Odyssey* (Rainbow Books, Aberdeen) was as follows:

I hope this neatly produced paperback, modestly priced, will be recognised as one of the important Scottish books of poetry of our time. Alastair Mackie has steadily developed in sustaining power, and in this collection he presents five poem-sequences of some length, all different, each well-constructed, with a variety of appropriate metres. In addition, it contains fourteen selections from his *Clytach* (Akros, 1972) and three later poems. It is ably illustrated with drawings by Frances Mackie, his daughter; these contribute to the book's impact, which is quite powerful.

Mr Mackie has the advantages of an Aberdeen upbringing among plain-spoken, hardworking, intelligent folk (the strong drawing of his father confirms this impression), and also of his present sojourn in Anstruther, where the Firth of Forth widens to the North Sea, and the Fifers' rich vocabulary augments that of his forebears. So his back-green commands a Homeric view (with due allowance for "ilers, coasters, seine-netters") and is a suitable place to read the Odyssey on a sunny day. There he meditates his title-poem.

Next comes "At the Back End" and "In the Thirties," followed by "Orpheus" in memory of Sydney Goodsir Smith, and the collection of sequences ends with "The Day-Book of a Death," almost unbearably moving in its plain, modern style: "...'for Jesus Christ, our Lord. Amen!' / We left him to get on with his death." It is dedicated thus: "For my father Frank Mackie, Quarryman (1901-1978)."

A death in the poet's family is a most difficult subject for him to attempt, at length, and with such direct treatment: the pressure of poetry to get itself written needs to be exceedingly strong. Everything is here: "Papers for birth, papers for death...," all these details of *La pompe funebre* that have to be filled in correctly. And meanwhile:

> Next cubicle a man canna mind
> the date o his weddin.
> He's registerin the birth
> o his first bairn.

Compare this with the stern, heart-rending effect of a more private stanza:

> Nor did I greet for you. Only your hirstlin
> oot your life in a ward bed
> hung ower me like a spaedom
> ye wid in time mak true.

Sydney Goodsir Smith impressed us mightily with his re-handling of the Orpheus story. Mr Mackie's sequence performs the same feat quite differently, beginning his narrative in solemn stanzas of fourteen lines with the effect of pentameters, followed by dialogue in a more urgent metre. The sections of speech by Orpheus and by Euridice vary the metres further and add to the impact of their separate personalities. We feel the strain of the man and the shade struggling to exist in the darkness. An element of the story quite new to me is the "scientific" explanation of Orpheus' music reacting with darkness to form the substance of Euridice:

> ...
> and the haill work wid body the beginnin
> and the end, till the kent face o his music
> kyths at last and dark's bairn is born.

A good poet uses anything from his memory that suits his purpose: in his Thirties sequence, Mr Mackie tells of his admiration "as a loun" for Boris Karloff. "He aye cam to life in a sotter o test-tubes, twirly wires..." This set of eleven poems is placed in the middle of the five sequences, giving a basis to all. Indeed, the whole book is well constructed. My favourite in this group is "Primary Teachers," "teuch weemin" with their "Lochgelly soond," whose "learning" (i.e. teaching, not their erudition) has stood the poet in good stead.

Mr Mackie is blessed with the ability to make good poetry out of material ready to hand, as well as plenty of "faur-ben" thoughts. The title-sequence makes use of the back-green, where he has taken his Homer, and by an easy metaphor he becomes Odysseus, though with frank misgivings — "I'm nae Ulysses and never will be. / The unkent is the next poem...," mixed with thoughts of Sir Patrick Spens, wrecked on his way to the Firth of Forth. With easy skill he inserts translations from Du Bellay and Mallarmé, very well-made too: "Ach, flesh is dowie and I've read all the tomes" — "La chair est triste, helas! et j'ai lu tous les libres" (Mallarmé: "Brise Marine"), and the whole sequence ranges widely from his back-green, suggesting that Mr Mackie has the staying-power for large-scale works.

"At the Back-End" serves as an Autumn sequel to "Back-Green Odyssey," though now he has Pushkin in his thoughts: "This is my season, like yours, Pushkin. / Let's see the hairst that I can gaither in."

Mr Mackie has thus deliberately gathered his hairst from a wide experience of life, and of places and books. He is a master of words and poetic forms. Felicities abound; I could not give a proper notion of these without a great many examples. He is a master especially of Scots, regarding this as his duty — "For gin it dee for ever...Scotland maun be cast oot into the backet o history...." But this duty is no burden: it helps him on his road. We sense this, throughout these five poem-sequences, and in the other seventeen poems I have not mentioned in particular. In a warm-hearted Foreword, Alastair Mackie expresses gratitude to all who helped him during his apprenticeship in poetry, including, no doubt, those "steam-hemmers," his primary teachers. But now he carries his Master's Ticket.

— *Words*, Autumn 1980

[To Hamish Henderson]   9 Nov 80

That was a remarkably fine and unusual television programme, especially unusual, I mean, in being built around and upon your *Elegies*, sort of, poems plus illustrations, not the other way about, and similarly it is rather uncommon to have books of poetry with illustrations, though Alastair Mackie's new book, *Back-Green Odyssey* has drawings that add to the effect of the book. All the same, to have illustrations from the Desert is really something. And anyone could see from the pictures what the Desert was like; there was no need for you to rub it in, and neither you did. That made what you had to say about the massacre in Rome that much more powerful. The production moved very fast, too, with Cambridge in about two scenes, and those pictures of the Pioneers, and all the way to Rome. I liked that cheerful party of former partisans. It

93

upset me a lot to see that inscription on the modern traffic-sign: very effective television to spot it and get it into the picture, but it did make me wish I hadn't seen it, and could have gone on thinking swastikas belonged to long ago. Curious it was the Jerry sign, in Italy, still. "The Banks of Sicily" came into its place in fine style, and the story belonging to it, in the place where it happened.

Well, anyway, it was a quite extraordinary programme, I mean, compared with the patterns of television. And yet there was nothing unusual in taking a writer to talk in the places he wrote about. But this one was different.

PS — You may wonder at it, but I was extraordinarily affected by the view of King's College, remembering Peg there with me on holiday. Right enough, though it came at the beginning of the film, not after all those big events.

Note: the film discussed here is *The Dead, The Innocent*, a TV programme about HH's war-time poems and songs. It was first broadcast on BBC2 on 8th November, 1980.

[To J. B. Caird]   1 Dec 80

...This has been a wearifu day, following the St Andrew's Night + MacCaig's birthday at the Grosvenor Hotel, which was a very good affair, very good indeed, and Iain C Smith had come from Oban, and Sam MacLean from Paris, where he had been giving a reading of his poetry and came home only the day before. (Curious thing I've noticed — the *cadence* in Sam MacLean's speech. Is it from Gaelic or from the delivery of ministers in Raasay?). But it started at 7.45 and when 11.45 came round it was still going strong and was apparently able to do so for an hour or so more. I became really terribly tired in the middle, or rather not far from the beginning of the second-last item, after which MacCaig was billed to come up for the third time. This second-last performer we had heard in the first of the evening's three halves, a chap with a guitar and a big repertory of mostly I think propaganda and sort of protest or rallying songs. It was his first song of this second appearance that I could not put up with any more, and the breaking-point came with a line about the Huns with their long-distance guns. Apparently history was being traced backwards; we had the Spanish Civil War in the first half, and maybe by a quarter past midnight we could be treated to the Battle of Inverkeithing. (What can be expected of an entertainment sponsored by the John MacLean Society?) So muttering apologies like holy water on all sides I steered between the tables and out. . . .

M. Moulton lent me the MacDiarmid symposium, and some of it interests me very much. Murison abounds with information about where MacD found his words and phrases, mostly from Jamieson and Chambers, and acknowledges the valuable findings by Ruth MacQuillan anent the latter. Scholars had been baffled, apparently, searching much less obvious sources in vain. Even more revelatory is Kenneth Buthlay on the sources of *To Circumjack Cencrastus*, a work I never could make anything of (and in fact didn't find interesting enough to try very hard, thinking vaguely for about 20 years or so that Circumjack was Cencrastus the Snake's Christian name, and that this was one of these many poems addressed to somebody or something, like "To a Mouse"), and it is no wonder I could make so little of it, considering that so much of it is versified from prose translations in English, e.g. of "a conversation with Valéry reported by Lefèvre," or of "T. E. Hulme paraphrasing Bergson," or of Nigel MacNeill's prose summary of Alasdair MacMhaighstir's verse. The "four pennies of Drimisdale" turn out to be parcels of land, like the pennylands of e.g. Caithness, and so on. Regarding Athikte, K. Buthlay says, "Never having heard of Athikte myself, I once asked MacDiarmid" who gave him an answer that was wrong in three particulars, only MacD remembered at least it was from Valéry. Sometimes, it appears, the scholar's search for clues is made easier if he can discover which books MacD had been sent to review shortly before he wrote a certain passage. Reading this, it did occur to me that while you have the chance the best thing to do is perhaps to ask the elusive poet himself. But maybe that would count as an academic foul and spoil the game. Such a thing happened to Peg, who learned (I forget how) that a scholarly lady was doing research into one of the last descendants of the French royal family (or so she claimed to be) and it happened that Peg knew this royal lady, who was known in Hampstead as The Princess. So, Peg wrote to the scholar, and it was very interesting, and much research was done into the validity of the Princess' claim. It was taken for granted that the Princess was dead long ago, and then she rather spoiled the fun by being found in a nursing-home somewhere, quite able and willing to tell her story, which was true enough. But a book was written, and the scholar gave Peg a copy with thanks, and it was very interesting, and Peg was pleased, and I have the book still. Opal Whitely, the Princess was called. It is a wonderful adventure story and apparently true.

So it does seem maybe more useful though less scholarly to ask the author so long as you have the chance. Though admittedly you may get a dim or even crafty reply. But in the case of Cencrastus, etc, I strongly feel, "Why bother?" And I don't see that MacD really made such skilful use of his unquoted quotations as people make out, even such notable people as Sorley MacLean (who told me that Grieve knew next to no Gaelic [not his own words]), nor N. MacCaig, who can be penetrating enough, but *does seem* to be impressed by attributes of MacD that are not there at all, so far as I can see, or by his behaviour, that looks very like antics to me. In fact, I weary of that deflated windbag, so unreliable as to say that Social Credit could easily make us all millionaires to-morrow, or was it the next day? — I forget. Millionaires we might all have been, according to Grieve's (not Douglas's) opinion, but we would have been just like those German millionaires of the twenties. As a man interested in Social Credit long ago, I imagined only a state of affairs that would give us all the means of subsistence, and if we were more ambitious (or our wives and children) some productive employment would give us a bit more purchasing power. And, in a major poet, I should expect to find a love and mastery of the sounds, meanings and influential/co-operative properties of words:

> Here at the heicht o' her dance
> Athikte's off in a dwam
> —Gane in a kink
> And no' able to think
> By what mischance
> She's tint her "I am"...(*Complete Poems*, p. 233)

Anyway, I'm sorry I kept ye our of yir bed so late, and forgot to call your attention to the spare blankets. And yet it gives me pride that people should come and stay in my house. Note the singular pronouns, alas!

Thank you, and Mrs. Mackie, for the Christmas card, a good one too, with a note about Botticelli on the back of it, very interesting; I'm sorry his popularity declined in the end, because of Leonardo da Vinci and Michelangelo, but that sort of thing can't be helped. And I wonder about his ambiguous attitude towards Savonarola, whom I took to be an all-or-nothing man with regard to both sending and receiving. But I have seldom, never, rather, had a card worth keeping because of its inclusion of a manuscript poem. I appreciate that. It is remarkable to observe, what is done with the end of her goun. I never noticed before that Mary is not in blue and white, as I have noticed from her graven images in R.C. schools. There is another card, by David, with a blue cloak and dark blue goun and a bit of red showing underneath. Once more I have noticed to my surprise something that everybody regards as familiar, like the days of the week? At my time of life too! Awell, it keeps me interested. I am disappointed that the Rainbow Books don't seem to have done what they ought to have done. I thought they were doing a good work. Well, so they are, I daresay, *considering*. There is no doubt that the publishing of Scots is still a sair fecht, but getting better, I think a little. I am glad you are doing it, anyway, and it vexes me that *Back-Green Odyssey* has not made such a noise in the world as should happen with a book of such importance as I think it is, anyway. Maybe it has; I hope it has. The review in *Words* may help, but I should have liked to be asked to review it for the T.L.S. (though I don't want to reduce *Words*). I don't see why not, considering how conductive the Border is. The word *skellies* is on page 4, in the fourth bit of "Back-Green Odyssey." I remember it because [Please forgive sudden gear-change. It is now Friday afternoon (it had no forenoon, because I slept-in till nearly noon {a luxury I used to daydream about when I was holding down a job} and it is now 5 to 3 and I have only just finished my dinner of soup and to-morrow's breakfast, not having had time to cook to-day's dinner in time for to-day's dinner-time, which took place punctually at 1 o'clock {I wonder about the possibility of ending a line thus...punk- and of starting the next line with -tilious — some people are too clever by half — }) but what I meant to tell you was, and still is, that I have found a nativity picture (a reproduction, that's to say) by Murillo, in which Mary is depicted wearing a reid goun and a blue-black coat over it. There must be some established procedure about this that I don't know about.] There is another thing I hastily did last night before going out to post a letter to somebody in Dundee University who asked me to take part in a poetry-reading on Feb 12th. I suggested to Val Warner, who had written to me, that if she wanted another Scots poet to take part in such a reading, she should have you in mind. I hope that is not something you would not have wanted me to do; I don't suppose so, only I notice your name is not in the Arts Council list of people who may be invited to take part. . . .

Yes, the skellies — I was going to say I remember being interested in this name for the rocks at Anstruther when I visited Forbes MacGregor at his house on the shore next to the harbour, as far as I remember: the old manse. Also I asked Mr. Murison if it was a variant of skerries and he was non-committal. Maybe there is a vexed question here. I don't know. It is now 7 p.m. and meanwhile I have shown the three Christmas cards I was on about, one of which he sent me, to Mr. Monaghan, and he also did not know about these colours, and became greatly interested. He is an art-teacher at Linlithgow. I have got on well with him for a long time. We used to come home in the same bus on Fridays, and got into the habit of having a cup of tea in a café and still do nearly every Friday. He liked your card, too, and also your poem about it, and he thought a good deal about its idea of the dark cloak as a howe-hole in the picture. He thought it might not have been so dark when the picture was new. But it is a striking thought about the picture as it is. The poem's ending is very fine. He thought the thatched roof looked familiar, yes, he thought, Botticelli's Studio. He was interested also in your sonnet as I described it, about Cézanne's apples. I shall show it to him. Between the last full-stop and the new capital (and between two parts of a concert by 3/4 of the Amadeus Quartet, the reason, I confess, why I had the wireless turned on at all, I listened to a programme about Herbert Read. I did not know he was such a good poet, and this is something which keeps happening. Ask any Edinburgh person of my lot and you are likely to be told that he ran off with one of his Fine Art lady-students. But was she pleased? The authorities were not, but what of it? His last poem, which was read, was about his wife, to the effect that (if I don't let it down) she was in all ways good to everyone around, though in no way out of the ordinary. And more and more I see the value of the "mediocre," so much despised by certain great people whose value declines in my judgment by several degrees every year or even month. Anyway, if you are thinking it is not right that I should stop pen-pushing only because the Amadeus 3/4 (one is unwell) were having an interval, I am of the same way of thinking. I had to stop after all and listen to that big Mozart Divertimento, and now feel more honest for that. But why? What Scottish past engenders that feeling? What Scottish modern humbug engenders that question? Anyway, your poetry is free from humbug, and so far as I can make out, free from the necessity of winning free of it. This house has a peculiarity: Peg, my wife, used to talk of the ghostly smells of cooking, or smells of ghostly cooking. We wondered if they came up to from downstairs. I have just been along the passage of B Deck to the Bog, or the Heads (to keep up the R.N. metaphor) and smelt without doubt the aroma of to-day's dinner (intended as to-morrow's breakfast: black pudding and ingans, a good experimental subject, easily identified). It is not in the kitchen, only in the passage. That reminds me of what I recollected, as especially in Benevento, in South Italy, site of the last battle of Guelphs and Ghibbelines (though why bother about them, when we were in prison and starving? {not a hunger strike like these terrorists who want P.o.W. status, just starving, that's all}) what, to me, presented itself as most powerfully evocative, deeply and even bottom-stirring, anguishing and at the same time extasising; in a word, beautiful, was T. S. Eliot's immortal:

"With smell of steaks in passageways"

[To Sydney Tremayne] 27 March 81

See this, and please excuse:

Lines

I hae a memory like a seeve.
It seeves the hairm frae the bien.
Hairm bides.
Bien rins doun the jaw-boax.
"Auld men forget."
Whae screivit thon generalitie?
I speak for masel.
Again-bite bides in the seeve.
Weill-duin is syndit awa.
I'm richt.
And I haenae the hairt to mak a poem o'd.

Well, I was cold-blooded enough to end a poetry-reading with that, to follow the expected procession of comical pieces. But the trouble is that I remember Peg's sore leg, and then her heart-trouble, and then her big trouble, all of which are so easy to understand mechanically. That mostly is why I'm always going on about the againbite of onwit, the remorse of conscience. But the other night I heard on the Open University . . . a lecture about decision-making, which finished with a remark that on looking back it is possible not to add remorse to regret, by thinking that, at the time, with the information that one had received, the decision was at least not so far wrong as it now appears: and that goes for the doctor who first took the view that Peg would just have to put up with her sore leg, and did not even look to see if there was anything about it that corresponded to anything he knew, and for all the resources of the Royal Infirmary and all.

The Masque of Edinburgh

THE MASQUE

OF

EDINBURGH

ROBERT GARIOCH

M. MACDONALD · EDINBURGH

1954

A POOPLICK LATTER, ODDRASH OR
MAUNAFASHTULE
By Guid Schir Skidderie Smithereens, *Barrelnut*

THUS SHPUKE HEE, impropertaeyou, a wee thingk effter the botching hoor o madnocht in a wale-kint and canspockle hous o cull somewhor in the sottie chitty, on the pabulicquatioun o this notetball dramma, as follios:

Nae Prodface thist, nobble Garioch, mine auld! Neigh mare cud I dashcrap it exunctuouslie ashk a Splore — na yet a Furorewud (yon's yure cowp-o-tay or pijoanie). It isna e'en an Introdrunctioun or yet a Bintrajunctioun. I kanna whatt in haill it isp nor yett whit it mocht soum bacchume, sae we'se jest bester doodle alang and spree and hump on the beast.

Man, guid sirs and life, gentile linties and shantymen, lollipopsies and jeelijaws, but it's a gey gad whane doun-sottins o the sin in spleendor sen fust the nobile, virtulous and galligant Geerioch-legionarius (*tunc in Italia captivus, eheu!*) receiptit (in totale fogsnoriance, bay it sod) yon profumous, maist preclarent and protomonsterous Bibicatioun o Carrotie's Fest Fowr Fetts — d'ye mind? Michtbe nocht, but til me tis jast leak yesthenicht.

Nou, in the coarse o the soif-samen Bibulocullatioun, your humile and maist sobredient varmint, the prosinct scraptor, did maist drouthicouthilie and rumsounduntinlie salude the sode Maister Rumboat Bleerioch's muchtie atomb (as thon it waste) o the *Bosque o Embro*, in the fooloweran weirds, gif my mammorie reculls collect, to wet and *fizz* (marrow leafs):

...this noncompareilaball unimitabolisticull ploy or dramantick excraution anent ure ain bromantick toun, this unmortall figmento (sune to be canplete efter the saccund sette o the nou enanepidemotic strait o aa-pervastive Barmageddoun be tenpyntorallie pistpotuit dew til the ramcunscionabull expanse invulvit) isht, washt and aye shell pea a praepotuant glaurie toll the wallowit num o this yauld crapitoul o the Hics and Sots, and a swird o the Lourd and o Bibeon for the cumflounderin o the pots of Belliall, the Moabitschitch wemen and the uncircumscissored Sumphs o Phoolistia that seick aye in Cauld Rakie hyresowl to dashcomfort, jurmummble and dumcrumbolize aa rantan lads, randie lassies and ilka rumprescunsiple gongrole baddie o scumdrie and obverse maens o luvelibrude frae gaddin abowt their lowful poccasions...*fib. stap.*

Man, hiv I no troken the beerie wads out my ain mowph! I cudnae sade it batter mamzel! I sollumlute ye, sir! Ye're a brainless

◀ The title-page of *The Masque of Edinburgh* published in 1954 wauner, sae y'are tae, a werrie brimless limmer! Uh mun ut. Oah moan oat. Ill rillie dill. Man maun rut. Onust. Inisht. Unch. Hipskittelantilie.

Ay, butt latt us be specious nou, spurious I mant. No, bott hair! Haud on procul! Cull me nae culls, cullie, or U'll bull ye! Dearyskoll, marysqueal, all the pretties fritties kill! You slay me, chick! For the luve o Dan gath askalon wi the buzznotes!...Ay, ye're rocht! Nou!

As I wash shprayan, whan I sae lewdlie intorumptit mumskull, it wale be clarilie gnotisoluble til the bleeriest licktor or boke-lunk, on tearin the follyant blawds, liefs or pashes, that the prosinct humbile scraptor or bintrodrunctor was a sooth Prumphatt inleid, for the grote Glaurirokh hasht echtyillie nou queyntpleatit and funushut the fumous *Musk of Adamanevenbroch* (or fatoxter he cracks the thingk), as yalla sun sea for yersail overluff.

For awe thatt and numbthelass, it wale be openanavident till the mimmest untalliginse that this wee fashiscull, opishcreel, or labellium macht wahl be meerilie the bedgunnin o an ommanse sago or soggy, for thor's nae ostendentional ondt tule the ploy; crappabile o inforanite expunsioun, it can braizilie gong on for over and over, this prossitutivelie and varytipple revelutioun sweitcaisse o a dramme, this harmonium-growtherum o the foolies and mildews o Edenborg, sotty o the sabbin houls, "ye cauld-kail toun," as the dramantickist himsole hash it.

Ach wole, juicit souke it an sweel, gintail licktor, as the Bish sot tuil the bint, and syne crup bock for mehrd. I'se warand yi'll no be dashaprunctit. Garioch, I solute ye! Lang may your lim rake! May your key niver want the queehole! Gomeril ruder, ride on!...

Quod SCHIR SKATTERIE, *as the knock strak. Teem, shantymen, plukes! Teem, nou! Teem!*

PREFACE

FIR the proper performance o this gigantic spectacle it will no be easy ti find a biggin big eneuch. The El Dorado in Leith micht dae at a pinch, but A'd raither hae the Waverley Market; the baith o thae places indeed are jist raither low in the roof, an it micht be better ti hire Leith Central Station. That wud dae fine, efter a wheen alterations. It micht be dune wi 3-D wi an extry-big screen and stereoectoplasmic soond, if that's whit they cry it. Hooiver, as it's mair likely ti be performit in a kirk haa somewhair, it can be managed wi a gramophone an lood-speaker, wi a wee knob for screwin the music up and doon, a big limelight contraption wi a whirligig ti birl forenenst the lens, and a tunin-fork. Whan the magneeficent scenic effects are needed, the Guide will tell the folk what they are supposed to see, and the whirligig maun be birlit ti mak a dazzle owre the stage. Whit's mair, whan ye come ti the words "A hush faws owre the hale affair" on Page 37 [130], the whirligig-dazzle will gie a chance for everybody ti get aff the stage binna the Makar an the Heilanman. Try that, onywey, an guid luck t'ye.

TIL

THIS MASQUE'S REVIVER

SYDNEY GOODSIR SMITH

MAISTER O ARTS AND MAKAR O POEMS

AUREATE AUKTOR

LUG-BEGUILFOU AUK

CREATOR O CAROTID CORNUCOPIUS

A DEEP DRINKER

FRAE THE PIERIAN SPRING

AGANIPPE AND SANCT BERNARD'S WELL

THE SAUT IN EMBRO'S PARRITCH

BERIALL BARD

PERLE IN POETRIE AND CRISTALE AMANG CRITICS

CHAIRBUNKLE O SCOTIA'S DARLING SEAT

THIS WARK IS DEDICAT

THE MASQUE O EDINBURGH

*THE PLOY begins wi the curtain up. The stage is tuim, wi nae
scenery, but decently hingit aboot wi draperies. There is a poupit or
lectern on yin side, wi a wee licht o its ain for the Guide ti read wi.
It wud be as weel ti stert wi three lood chaps on the flair, seein
there's nae curtain tae histe up.*

Enter the Official Guide
*[Ye ken fine wha he is, because he has a muckle roon medal sort o
thing wi the inscription:* OFFICIAL GUIDE. *It maun be big eneuch for
the folk ti read it frae the gallery. He cairries twa mair placards and
hings them on the draperies. Tane reads:* AITCHESON HOUSE *and the
tither:* TOON MUSEUM. *He taks up his position ahint his lectern,
switches on his wee licht, an says his piece.]*

GUIDE
*An noo, Leddies an Genlemen, we're at the tap end o the Canogait,
or whit's left o the Canogait onywey. Jist up the road there's a guid
wee howff cried the Ne'ergate, in memory o the Nethergate Port
that stude thair till it was dingit doon ti mak wey for the traffic.
Doun the road is the site o Sludge the Medium's memorial
fountain. It was dingit doon because it was gaun ti faw doon
onywey. The auld Canogait Cross stude thair an aa, but folk said it
didny luik richt withoot the fountain, sae they shoved it inside the
kirkyaird oot o the wey o the folk comin hame on a Se'urday nicht.
Even yet, some o them try ti lean on it oot o habit, and they get an
awfie suck-in when they find it's no thair.*

Enter Donald *[got up ti look like yin o the auld Toon Guaird, wi
a Lochaber axe an aw. He glowres aboot him a whilie, syne stauns
at ease like a sentry fornenst the Museum.]*

GUIDE
*This is the latest ploy o the Toon Cooncil's, specially ti please the
towrists.*

107

[addresses the audience] Whit d'ye think A'm supposed ti be?
The last o the Toon Guaird. This is the Toon Museum, and A'm
Exhibit A. They've pitten me here as a kinna historical ornament
for an ancient monument. It suits me fine. A'd raither be
ornamental nor yisfy ony day.

Enter the Makar *[in poortith's ain claes, gey mauchy an duddy,
his lang hair staunin strecht abuin his heid, a grubby lookin ticket
whan awse duin; an airmfy of buiks gruppit ablow his oxter.]*

MAKAR

[ti Donald] Guaird...Shun!
*[Donald tries ti cairry oot the order. He haunnles his Lochaber axe
like a sodger wi a rifle. This is no that easy, as it is seeven or echt
feet lang.]*

MAKAR

Guaird...Preesent airms!
*[Donald does his best, but he lets his wappon faw wi a clatter. The
Makar picks it up.]*

MAKAR

Ech, Donald, ye'll never mak a sodger. Hoo d'ye like yer new
job?

DONALD

I suits me fine. A sham sodger in a sham capital. Nice for the
towrists.

MAKAR

[He hauns Donald back his axe.] Here, tak a haud o this thing.
There's somebody comin.
*[Ye hear a distant merch on the Pipes. It gits looder an looder while
the Makar says his piece, bit no that lood thit ye canny hear him.]*

MAKAR

Guid save iz, here's a Heilanman
merchin up the Bridges
wi a *sgean dubh* in his stockin an
a claymore in his haun;

yech! hoo're ye feelin, man,
breengin wi the fidges
ti speir gin Embro's waukin? —
an he says he's feelin graun.

Stravaigin owre the ridges
o mony-valleyed Edinburgh,
owre-valued Edinbro, yon cauld-kale toon
thit glowres doon her nose —
her neb thit's aye rinnin
whan the east-wun blows —
at an ill-bred loon
wha maun aye be sinnin,
sayin "blaws" insteed o "blows."

Fegs! here's a Heilanman
traipsin up the Bridges
wi a pen stuck in his stockin an
a notebuik in his haun;
hech! hoo're ye. . .

Enter Heilanman *[a wycelike callant in Harris tweed, a braw big
sawmonflee stuck in his hat.]*

HEILANMAN
Pardon me, but could you be directing me to the University?

MAKAR
A sud think sae. A'm a student thair masel. And Donald here is a
graduate wi First Cless Honours.

HEILANMAN
Edinburgh is indeed a city of learning. My teacher in
Clachnaskeechan used to tell me that the very doorkeepers and
porters were Masters of Arts.

MAKAR
He wisnae that faur oot. Mebby jist the wrang wey roon. Maist o
the Maisters o Arts feenish up as porters and doorkeepers.

DONALD
Or chuckers-oot in the pubs.

109

HEILANMAN

Or schoolmasters?

MAKAR

Aye, bit ye maun be gey teuch fir that job.

HEILANMAN

[ti Donald] Are ye really an M.A. yourself?

DONALD

Aye, an A can preive it. Hae ye fand Jock Hewieson's Bar on yer traivels?

HEILANMAN

No, I have not had time to see many of the public buildings.

DONALD

Ye'll find it aw richt. And whan ye gang in, tak a look at a wee broon cylinder amang the boattles, on the skelf ahint the bar. Thon's ma Graduation Scroll.

HEILANMAN

And what is it doing there at all?

DONALD

Aweel, we had a bit o a celebration in Jock Hewieson's the nicht o the Grad., an A pit it thair ti be safe. A haena fand a use fir it syne, sae thair it bides. It gies the howff a kinna intellectual look, an it's an unco guid example ti the students.

MAKAR

It's a fine graduate you are.

DONALD

A'm aw that. And whit aboot yersel? A keelie by origin, a student by designation, a makar by natur an a drouth by choice. Product o a thoosan years o Scottish culture.

MAKAR

[ti Heilanman] An whitna career hae ye got in mind fir yersel?

110

HEILANMAN

I'll study for my degree.

MAKAR

Aye.

DONALD

Aye.

HEILANMAN

Then I'll attend Moray House.

MAKAR

Aye.

DONALD

Puir felly!

HEILANMAN

Then I'll be a teacher in a fine school in Inverness or in Edinburgh, yes, or maybe in London herself. And maybe some day I'll have a holiday in the hotel at Clachnaskeechan, along with the other gentlemen who go there for the fishing.

MAKAR

It's a graund ambeetion.

HEILANMAN

Yes, it will be a fine change from the crofting.

DONALD

Ma graundfaither was a teacher in a wee skuil in Badenoch. An ma faither's a professor o Philosophy. Sae ma present job is a kinna logical conclusion, as ye micht say.

HEILANMAN

You have a strange turn of speech, considering your origins.

DONALD

Aye, an it took a bonny lot o practice, A can tell ye. A carried on ma extra-mural studies maistly in Jock Hewieson's. Noo A can speak Canogait geynear like a native. It wad be weel if mair folk wad dae likewise. Insteed o that the Embro folk try ti talk Mayfair, an feenish up wi Morningside.

But you haven't told me about the University.

Och, it's aw richt fir a wheen weelbrochtup folks wi minds like their unremarkable Sawbath suits an as sleepy as Johnnie Cope, bit A doot they need some o your kind ti wauken them up a bittie. The Embro folk are aw asleep in the airms o Sir Walter, an gin ye dinny gant awaw wi the lave, they runkle their nebs that wey ye'd think ye'd gotten the stink o hell-reek about ye. Ye're gaun ti the University, are ye? See thit ye traivel by Pelman Coach, an dinny think owre muckle, or dae onything eccentric in ony ither kind o wey, an ye'll dae fine. A'll gie ye a wee recite anent Edinburgh, the centre o Scotland's wealth o culture.

This is the cue for Scots Music: "Scotia's Glory," a selection o Scottish airs wi brilliant variorums, rendered by Maister Hamish Smith (16) and his wee sister Morag (13½). A real waterfall splairges aboot the stage, amid the mists o a real Heilan glen. The Makar recites his wee poem.

A makar in a Woolworth tie
an siven-an-sixpenny flannen breeches
may reid the mirky midnicht sky
an buiks o Eliot's an Neitzsche's.

Gowpin an glowrin in the Lyft,
he kens a hantle o shooblimity,
an ettles sair ti mak a shift
o tummlin tae the Haly Trinity.

Syne, bizzin up in P.T.'s lift,
a man wi dozent, sonsy face
reveals a mind o queerer drift:
Nearer, ma Gode, ti Thee, he says.

112

Burns fand a moral, coupin mice,
an Wordsworth socht religion in a stirk.
Gode warks in maist mysterious weys;
A've kent folks even seek it in a kirk.

Wha'll blame me, syne,
or slate this clarty dialect o mine?

A camel in the desert'll
slorp drumly watter oot a dub;
a man wha'd write in Edinbro
maun seek his language in a pub.

Thir's been some queerlike cheenges in the toon,
nae SHEPHERD noo eats eysters by the gross;
it's no the thing thae days ti sweel it doon
wi Dawny Douglas in the Anchor Close.

The lave o us hae usquebae,
Craigmillar yill and eau-de-vie;
a makar cudny but be gay
in sic a crousie company.

It's no si queer as some wud think
that poetry suld gang wi drink.

William Dunbar himsel set glesses clinkin
an kent the awfy drouth thit comes o thinkin.

Did Burns no find *his* choicest cavern
in this same Dawney Douglas' Tavern?

Did Burns no read, or he micht taste:
LORD · IN · THE · IS · AL · MY · TRAIST.*

The lintel-stane o Bacchus' Court:
THE · LORD · IS · ONLY · MY · SVPORT.*

Twa gowden texts abuin a howff,
symbol in whilk the truth may dern?

But wheesht noo, fegs!
A think A've tummilt tae the hale concern!

---

* Thae letterit lintels were in Anchor Close at the time whan the verses
were screivit, bit they were dang doon langsyne and biggit intill a waa in
the Canogait, near Aitcheson House.

This Edinburgh's jist a bag o tricks
filled tapsleteerie baith bi Gode and Deevil,
maist recent acquisitions being Auld Nick's
(or Satan's raither, no ti be unceevil.)

The bust o Socrates in Riddle's Court,
gin he cud speak, ma coanscience, hoo he'd scorn iz;
King Chairlie's yaud, prancin owre Knox's grave,
a pliskie in the very style o Hornie's.

The Royal Mile, gane rotten like oor teeth,
the breakers' men ding whummle doon aboot iz;
St. Giles got up in nice Victorian claes:
twa nesty bits o handiwark o Clootie's.

The Usher Hall, frae foons o honest beer
risen, bi grace o Gode, a guidly hicht,
slockens oor sauls fir saxpence (Upper Tier)
Bach an Beethoven on a Sawbath nicht.

Oor Scottish claes are fine for deevils' tricks;
the feck o folk wha daur ti wear the kilt
maun be the kind wi shanks like parritch-sticks
while wycelike wichts gang breekt — the Deil's intillt.

Baritone Border reivers in braw dickies,
MacGregor's Gathering bawled by feckless nickies,
English-owned shops retailin tairtan gairters:
we'll suin see tairtan nickie-tams on cairters.

The floodlit castle, the romantic slums,
Oor Tounis College teachin fykes frae Thrums,
wi first-class honours gien tae donnert stirks
wha memorise professors' fisks and firks.

John Knox himsel gaes brawly wi the plan,
he gree'd wi Mary like a cat an moose;
noo Hollywood keeps up the dirrydan
wi talkin picturs richt firnenst his hoose.

Fake Yankee snufflin o denatured Scots
fechts wi fawse Mayfair o the middle-cless;
a makar is a rigglin mang stots,
fidgin wi virr, unsiccar o success.

Time merches on, but no in Edinbro,
Here Time adds up like an addeetion sum;
naething is lost. Holyrood, Knox's hoose,
Mary and Knox thersels, the muckle lum

at Portobelly; gasworks, breweries,
the castle, Princes Street, the Canogait
wi aw the folk whaw hae adae wi them
are mixed thegither, indiscriminate.

A've seen masel, abuin a score o times,
Burns, Ramsay, Fergusson gang airm-in-airm,
glowred-at by polis an the auld toon-guaird;
it's nocht bit glawmerie, but whit's the hairm?

GUIDE

*During the last verse or twa, we've been hearing the Toon Guaird's
tune, "Jockie to the Fair," an noo it gets gey loud as some chiel
screws up the lood-speaker ahint the scenes. A procession o Toon
Guaird, as mony as possible, say ten, tho a hunner wad mak a
better show, is seen approachin up the passage-weys o the
auditooraloorum. They gang throu some pseudo-military drill,
watched by Donald, the Makar and the Heilanman, wha look as
gin they were seein ghaists.*

DONALD

Here! Div ye see whit A see?

HEILANMAN

I do see it. And I don't like it at all, at all. My grandmother who
had the second sight saw...

MAKAR

Listen ti whit A'm tellin ye. Bit ye're no listenin. That's jist the
kinna thing that happens ony day in Edinburgh. Ye'll git yaised
wi'd eftir a whilie.

GUIDE

*The procession forms up in a military mainner, mair or less.
[Donald finds himsel staunin awkwertly in front. The sergeant
notices him.]*

SERGEANT
Hey, you long trink of water there. Fall in, will you not?

DONALD
Ach, awa wi ye!

SERGEANT
Away with me is it? Fall in pefore I haff you on a charge. Fall in!
*[Donald falls in, richt in the centre o the front rank, shovin awa
the men ti mak room for himsel.]*

SERGEANT
Guard, number!
*[They number awa as they are telt, coontin up tae, say, eleeven. If
we stertit wi a hunner, they will coont up tae a hunner an yin.]*

SERGEANT
Eleven? There were only ten when we left the guard-house.

MAKAR
Aweel, they're jist leevin up tae their bye-name. The toon-
rottans, they're weel-named.

SERGEANT
Toon-rottans, is it?

MAKAR
Rottans, aye, or rats gin ye want it in English. They've bred
anither on the road.

SERGEANT
I know you well. You're Robert Fergusson the makar. Ye'll mak
some ponnie verses in the guard-house this night. I'll put you in the
plack hole, see that I don't.
*[He sets his men ti nab the Makar. There is a guid-gaun bicker.
Donald taks pairt on the Makar's side. In the end the Makar hauds
them aff wi a blaud o raither dirty paper.]*

MAKAR
Aye, an these same verses will set the hale toon lauchin at ye the

morn. Wad ye like a wee tait o ma tawse? I scrievit this in yer honour the nicht afore last.
[He reads Fergusson's verses.]

> And thou, great god o acquavitae
> Wha sway'st the empire o this city,
> When fou, we're sometimes capernoity,
>   Be thou prepared
> To hedge us frae that black banditti
>   The City Guaird.
>
> Oh sodgers, for yer ain dear sakes,
> For Scotland's, alias Land o Cakes,
> Gie not her bairns sae deidlie paiks
>   Nor be sae rude
> Wi firelock and Lochaber axe
>   As spill their blude.

That's jist a wee prayer, in a mainner o speakin. You gar yer men grup me, and A'll try ma haun at a curse.

SERGEANT
Chust so, chust so. Guard, fall in!
[They form up as before.]

SERGEANT
[ti Makar] Well, well, you haff done nothing this time, put don't do it again. The Town-guard iss a famous force, and not to pe laughed at.
[The Sergeant taks the Makar aside wi him in a secretive kinna mainner, an produces something like a stalk o rock a yaird lang. It has a label on it: DYNAMITE.*]*

SERGEANT
What would you say to the idea of plowing up the Tollbooth?

MAKAR
A hadnae thocht o that, but it's a gey guid idea.

SERGEANT
Here you are, then. The ferry thing you need.

[The Makar taks the dynamite. It has anither label on the back: GOVERNMENT SURPLUS — DUMMY. *For the rest of the ploy he cairries this thing aboot wi him.]*

SERGEANT
[Speakin ti the company in general.]
There wass a Town Guard in Edinburgh in the time of the Romans.

MAKAR
Aye, and ye wad be in it, likely.

SERGEANT
Yess, I wass. Old soldiers neffer die. I wass here when Chulius Caesar marched into Edinburgh.
[Makar taks the Heilanman's airm an leads him over to hae a word wi Donald.]

MAKAR
Dis this no beat aw? We'll be haein Julius Caesar wi us neist.

DONALD
Caesar niver cam near Edinburry.

MAKAR
Ach, that's aw yin tae the Embro folk. Caesar niver in Embro! They'll no staun fir that, man.

GUIDE
Pseudo-Roman military music is heard gettin nearer and, of coorse, looder. A kenna whit it suld soon like, but neither will ony o the audience either. Or if ony o them happen ti ken, we'll be muckle obleeged fir ti be pitten wise, and we'll hae the richt music for the neist performance.

Enter Caesar *[wi aboot a platoon o his men or sae. A Century in chairge o a Centurion wad look gey weel gin it cud be mainaged.]*

GUIDE
They gie us a display o drill in the Roman military style.

[ti 2nd Toon Guaird] What soldiers are these in the strange kilt that has no pleats in it at all, and is not made of the tartan either?

2ND TOON GUAIRD

I'm chust thinking they must pe the Romans.

IST TOON GUAIRD

An yess, the Romans they will pe indeed. And who is that man with the gret nose on him that is like the beak of an eagle?

2ND TOON GUAIRD

That will pe Chulius Caesar her nainsel.

IST TOON GUAIRD

What's he going to do now?

2ND TOON GUAIRD

He iss going to make a speech. They say he iss foreffer making the ponnie speeches.

CAESAR

Veni!

ALL

Hurray!

CAESAR

Vidi!

ALL

Hurray!

CAESAR

Vici!

ALL

Hurray! *[Lood an prolonged cheering.]*

CAESAR

Milites...Stannat...Ease!
[This suld be in Latin bi richts. Mebby the Producer micht fin oot the correct expression.]

119

CAESAR

Barbara celarent darii ferioque prioris.

1ST TOON GUAIRD

What did he say?

2ND TOON GUAIRD

If it iss the Gaelic he iss speaking, it must pe the East Country
Gaelic, for I know the West Country Gaelic well enough, and I
cannot make out a word.

MAKAR

Yon's no the Gaelic, ye muckle sheep's heid; it's the Latin. A
made oot something about the barbarians.

2ND TOON GUAIRD

He will pe telling them something about the Sassenachs, hooch
aye. They haff chust come here from Londinium.

DONALD

Wheesht! He's gaun tae speak again.

CAESAR

Cesare camestres festina baroco secundus.
Tertia darapti disamis datisi felapton.
Bocardo ferison habet —

ALL

Hurray!

DONALD

A keep thinkin A've heerd this afore sometime.

CAESAR

Quarta insuper addit.

ROMANS

[Groans.]

CAESAR

Bramantip camenes dimaris fesapo fresison.

Hurray!

SERGEANT

I must try to speak to him. I have a word of Latin I would like to try.
[Sergeant merches up ti Caesar and gies him a salute, smert eneuch.]

SERGEANT

Ave! Caesar.

CAESAR

Ave! Doochie.

SERGEANT

I did not think you would know my name, sir.

CAESAR

Have I not met you before? I was in the Highlands one summer, but I did not stay long. It rained all the time, and I did not get on well with the Caledonians. Do you know Haver McAver, the boatman of Gourock?

SERGEANT

Ho yess, she knows him weel. She wass his next neighbour's door.

CAESAR

[He faws intill a Heilant accent.]
Put you will pe...*[coughs]*. But you will be wondering what brought me to Edinburgh. I came to see if some of your men would join up in my bodyguard. We could do with some fine men like you.

SERGEANT

[Addressing the rank of T.G.] Do you hear this, my men? What do you say to choining Chulius Caesar's podyguard?

1ST TOON GUAIRD

Indeed, sir, I'll choin.

121

And so will I.

And so will I.

CAESAR

Splendid! splendid! A fine body of men.

SERGEANT

It will pe a fine change for us all. We're all used to podyguard duty. The last time it was Pontius Pilate's podyguard that we were in.

GUIDE

Fade in Pseudo-Biblical Eastern music. It grows louder, as ye may hae come to expect. Meanwhile all murmur crescendo *until there is a guid deal o noise awthegither.*
[The Makar taks the centre o the stage, hauds up his richt haun like a traffic-bobby, and shouts.]

MAKAR

Stop!
[Silence.]

MAKAR

A draw the line at Pontius Pilate. It's time we had a sang onywey. C'mon you and gieze a haun.
[Donald, the Makar, the Heilanman and the Sergeant form up in the front o the stage ti mak a quartette, Tenor I, Tenor II, Bass I, Bass II, or in the richt order for their voices onywey. Gin they canny sing they hae nae business ti be here, sae they'll jist hae ti dae their best. Whit's mair, they maun keep ti their ain pairts, and nae man maun sing ony kind o hauf-an-hauf or shandygaff.]

MAKAR

Let's hae a chord ti stert wi. *[He bangs a tunin-fork and gies oot the note Doh. Gin he's a tenor, the Bass II maun dae this, whaeiver he happens ti be. But, ach! the musical director can see ti aw this. A maun get on wi ma ploy. It's gettin fell near closin-time, an A'm no near feenished wi'd.]*

122

Gieze a guid chord, noo.

[They sing: Doh me soh do, tane efter tither, an haud on ti a guid chord, geynear in tune.]

MAKAR

[Sings. Tune: "The Ball o Kirriemuir"]
> A'll sing a sang, a sang, a sang
> that's neither short nor sweet
> anent historic Edinburgh,
> Scotia's darlin seat.

[Quartette, Donald, Makar, Heilanman, Sergeant, sing the chorus in fowre pairts.]

QUARTETTE
> Singin Whaes is it this time,
> Whaes is it noo?
> The yin that had it last time,
> He haesnae got it noo.

MAKAR

C'mon ye sodgers, jine in the chorus.

GUIDE

[To audience] That includes you an aw.

ALL
> Singin Whaes is it, etc.

DONALD
> Agricola the Roman
> cam here in Echty-three
> ti fecht the Caledonians
> an garr'd the callants flee.

QUARTETTE
> Singin etc.

SERGEANT
> Put soon the Caledonians
> who changed their names to Picts,

123

they chased the Romans oot again,
and gave them all their licks.

ALL
Singin etc.

HEILANMAN
The kingdom o Northumberland
reached tae the Firth o Forth;
but whan the Picts had dune wi it,
it wasnae that faur north.

QUARTETTE
Singin etc.

MAKAR
The Scots became a nation
wi borders on the Tweed,
wi toures an waas an battlements
for fear o Southron greed.

ALL
Singin etc.

DONALD
The Edwards cam a-reivin
to see whit they cud tak.
They stole oor Stane o Destiny
an wudnae gie it back.

QUARTETTE
Singin etc.

SERGEANT
Whan Bruce had chased them oot again,
and gien them scot fir lot,
they promised tae return the stane,
but somehoo they forgot.

ALL
Singin etc.

HEILANMAN

Whan Jamie Saxt o Scotland
went sooth in sixteen-three
he took the court tae London
an forgot his auld countree.

QUARTETTE

Singin etc.

MAKAR

But Cromwell did his very best
tae end that Royal breed;
he rigged a court o justice
an cut aff King Charles's heid.

ALL

Singin etc.

DONALD

Whan Cromwell cam tae Edinbro
he didnae steal a stane.
He stole the Scottish Records
an tae London they were taen.

QUARTETTE

Singin etc.

SERGEANT

They stawed them inty barrels
jist like a lot of junk
tae send them back by watter
but the maist o them got sunk.

ALL

Singin etc.

HEILANMAN

The lectern frae Holyrood
is big and unco braw,
but noo it's in St. Albans
for they've liftit it an aw.

Singin etc.

MAKAR

In Seeventeen-oh-seeven
the Parliament an aw
were wafted sooth frae Edinbro
an coffined in Whitehaa.

ALL

Singin etc.

DONALD

An sin they nabbed oor Parliament
the rest is nae surprise;
they come nae mair a-reivin,
noo they simply nationalise.

QUARTETTE

Singin etc.

SERGEANT

The Embro Electricity
saved up a million quid.
A chiel cam doon frae London,
said "I'll grab it," an he did.

ALL

Singin etc.

HEILANMAN

On Brabazons an puggy-nuts
oor bawbees dance a jig;
we'll get oor post-war credits
whan they bigg the Forth Road brig.

QUARTETTE

Singin etc.

MAKAR

Then comrades come, Raleigh,
Frobisher an Drake,

126

an aw the bonny pirates
wha stole for England's sake.

ALL
Singin etc.

DONALD
Come mak a braw procession
ti grace oor Scottish stage;
Gie three guid cheers tae greet the new
Elizabethan age.

[General cheering, etc.]

GUIDE
*Noo we hae a graund transformation scene. Edinburgh Castle is
pentit on a backcloth saxty feet in hicht, floodlit an aw. Frae the
toure that beilds the Bruce's crown flees the Royal Standard, wi
English quarterings as usual. Fireworks fizz aboot the Esplanade.
Chambers are dischargit wi shouts o Gardyloo. A lone piper comes
oot frae the yett o the Castle, followed by a Graund Symbolical
Procession o Historical Personages: Edward I wi a hammer,
Edward II wi a stane, Elizabeth I wi a chopper, Raleigh and Essex
wi their heids tucked underneath their airms, Hawkins wi a nigger
on a chain, Drake wi a barber's pole, Cromwell wi a sack o
wastepaper slung owre a bauble in the shape o a siller cosh, an aw
the Secretaries o State for Scotland in a chain gang, led by the
Mither o Parliaments an driven by the Auld Leddy o Threidneedle
Street. They jine hauns and sing "Ole Langzyne." Amid deefnin
applause frae assembled School-teachers and Beadles o the United
Free Church of Scotland (Continuing) the Castle scene rows itsel in
twa pairts, revealin John Knox's Hoose an a Movie Palace. The lyft
flichters, an cherubic boy-scouts flee aboot wi wings, kilts and
bagpipes. A stramush o bells an hooters appears drumlie on the
horizon, grows bigger an bigger, till it smores the hale stage in a
murky fug o hooters an bells.*

BELLS AN HOOTERS
Hootyall! Hootyall! Hootyall!

Honk! Honk! Honk! Honk!
Oh, listen to the band,
oh, listen to the band,
the mewsic transatlantically canned,
so transcendentalistically grand,
untouched by hand.

JOHN KNOX

*[Leanin frae the neuk o his hoose: a dourheidit divine wi
stiffstairched dogscollar.]*

LUVE · GOD · AND · THY · NICHTBOUR · AS · YISELF

MARY QUEEN O SCOTTIS

(laughs) Heeheehee, heeheehee,
(sings) Soolaytwa diparree.

JENNY GEDDES

Ye howlin Jezebel, ye! Ye bleatin priestess o Baal, ye! A'll kaim
yir noddle wi ma fauldstule, ye wi yer masses and yer collects. Deil
colic the wame o ye!

JOHN KNOX

Ay, ay, ma bonnie leddy, wi yer Frenche fillockis, fidlaris, an
others o that band. A jalouse, gin ye may git the hoose alane, thir
may be seen skippin no very cumlie for honest wemen.

MAKAR

Never ye mind, hen. Gie me yer airm.
[He taks her airm very gracefully.]

JENNY GEDDES

Hech sirs, did iver ye see the like o that? In braid daylicht tae!
*[She ups wi her faldstule an gies the Makar an awfie dunt on the
side o the heid thit gars his harns gang dirlin a bittie.]*

MARY QUEEN O SCOTTIS

Whit is't ails ye onywey...I can see nae hairm...
[She gaes aff in a dwam.]
Water...a drink o warrer...

128

[in grey strippit troosers, shepherd's tairtan plaid an a lum-hat wantin the croon.]
It's twalve an a tanner the boattle.

[in a guid complete suit o armour, gey duntit but wi nae chinks intillt.]
Eh, maister, wull ye gie me the address o yer spiv?

[in a demob suit the waur o the wear, an Angola sark an a Paris model high-grade hat.]
Ach man, stick tae the nappie at wan an six the pint.

The pint, did ye say? D'ye mean the pint Scots? Twa quarts English?

It's tippence a pint Scots at Maggy Johnston's on the Meedies.

An that's gey dear.

Your young men would be drinking, full stoups on the table, and horns of silver going round in their fists.

[A thrang o wee loons got up ti look like Auld Edinburgh Fishwives, Roupin-wives an Alewives, screech oot in a heich boygirlish skirl.]

News o Flodden! News o Flodden!
[A newspaper laddie comes rinnin wi his papers. He has a newsbill as lang as a streetch o waa-paper.]

Awfie ootrage in Edinburry. "Queen Elizabeth" sunk at Puddickie. St Andrew's Hoose blawn up by Toon Guaird. Calton Gaol demolished. Bang gaes saxpence.

I   129

A maist camsteerie widdle steers up the hale clamjamphrey. Zeinty Teinty, Tithery Mithery an Irky Pirky tak a tawrry rope an set aboot the Reverend John Thomson an the Very Reverend Jock Tamson. John Knox casts his duddies tae the wark wi shouts o "Heave awa lads, A'm no deid yet." Socrates, dancin the Mason's Apron an birlin widdershins, tichtens his tairtan nickie-tams an jines battle wi his faither's chisel. Up stours a Corporation fire-escape, crushing a nummer o Waiters, Tooncooncillors, Persons wi Nae Fixed Abode an Agents Provocateurs. The ladder zooms up in a monstrous erection, an in a break o the clouds, in a bleeze o licht, mid strains o "Land o (saft) Soap an Soddy" an "Scots wha Hqe," they see, climmin up the fire-escape thit leads ti Parnassus, John G. Smith, dux boy o George Watson's College, dressed as Sir Walter Scott, brandishin a copy o the "Merchant Maiden." They gaze, dumbstruck, as he grades towards Parnassus. Syne, ti the horror o mony prominent Educationists an ither cultured folk, he's cam ti the tap o the ladder wi Parnassus a gey lang bittie abuin his heid. He wabbles an wabbles an faws wi an acceleration o thretty-twa feet per second per second, per second square if ye'd raither hae it that wey, plump on tap o a Secondary Skuil English Teacher (Chapter V) sae that he dees.

[deein]
  Dem!
[dees]

A hush faws owre the hale affair. The stage dwines oot o sicht an the scene fades intill the licht o common day. The Makar an the Heilanman traipse slawly up the High Street, dodgin Corporation buses an wee laddies wi guiders. Their een insist on readin bills ootside shop windaes, displayed on hinging signs, danglin frae lamposts: WE GAVE SHOOTING-STAR 20-1, EDINBURGH TYPIST'S YO-YO RECORD, BANANAS THE ALLFOOD FRUIT, M.O.H. SAYS SPITTING SPREADS DISEASE. Chorus o wee loons an keelies singing "Auf Wiedersehen" and "Oo That Kiss!" Twa methsodden auld randies pu each ither's hair jist ootside a close. The Heilanman taks it aw in wi interest.

HEILANMAN
Tell me all about the Scottish Renascence.

MAKAR
Och, no in the High Street. A'm owre scunnert wi the place.
C'waw tae Jock Hewieson's an forget we bide in Edinburry.
[They gang aff the stage, airm in airm.]

GUIDE
Exeunt the Makar an the Heilanman, sober.

[The lichts fade awa. The Guide pits oot his ain wee licht an gaes aff frae ahint his lectern. The ploy is duin.]

131

Letters II

Extracts from SCOTTISH INTERNATIONAL REVIEW *editorial correspondence*

During the lifetime of *Scottish International Review* Robert Garioch acted as an advisory editor for the magazine and his initial responses to MSS submitted were written down as memos to Edwin Morgan and Bob Tait. Much of this material (which is now kept in St Andrews University Library) is by its nature fragmentary and none of it, of course, was intended for publication. With the permission of the trustees (Christopher Smout, Edwin Morgan, Bob Tait) I have selected a few items which show how Garioch reacted to some of the submissions.

(no date)

Stevenson. I would have this, just as it is, as a birthday tribute to F. G. Scott from the modern Scottish composer most eligible for the job. I would say we should do this out of respect for the authority and authoritarianism of H. MacD. and R. Stevenson, and for their prerogative and privilege in celebration of the birthdays of Burns and F. G. Scott. So everyone can see for himself how badly it is done. Some day we should ask some more unassuming and less close-to-God musicologist to give us a properly useful article on F. G. Scott, who never seems to be considered as he has a right to be. For my part, I have hob-nobbed enough with singers to ask them why they did not sing these songs more, and it seems that sometimes or often they find he does not give them the sort of vocal line that a singer wants.

4 Feb 68

Bernard Kodjo Laing. These poems have a real struggle going on in them, which is good poetry, even if they do not produce a clear message or communication or whatever you should call it. They have struggle and polish. I would vote for "Birthplace" mainly because of "I'm not available for abuse today," and the "are you" questions, and also because of the last three lines. But others may prefer "If You Dare to Swim," which is similarly good. We could hardly have two long ones, for practical reasons. I think "Let Trees

134

on Winter Food" is too puzzling, and would prefer "Get Rid of Social Death." Anyhow this man is a proper discovery.

27 Feb 68

George Bruce, "Nearly Always Summer." I should advise certainly send this to Callum right away. I like it very much, and so will a great many people whose interest we want to keep, and who will be puzzled by Stephen Bann; also I think many people will like both. This is in fact very well done: I don't know whether its method is planned or not, but it has the naturalness of someone talking, and yet I find it interesting all the time. It starts very well and arouses curiosity in what is going on and what Mr Finkelstein is up to: is he to be a figure of fun? Oh no, we discover, and he appears in the drawing-room, and so we are nicely started on the fish trade and the musical evenings.

12 March 68

Robert Nye, "Story of Sdeath." I do not think that this is any good. We used to show off by writing this sort of thing when we had just left the university, and I am not using the editorial we, I mean the whole gang of us. Take away the bits put in to upset Auntie and to please those who wish to dissociate themselves from her, and there is nothing left but an embarassingly familiar style.

Anne Stevenson, Poems. These stand out from all of this batch. Things operate on her sensitivity and interesting expressions come out. She does tend to go on too long.

15 Sept 68

Gaelic poems by Iain Crichton Smith and Derick Thomson. They all seem to be good poems, so far as I can tell by the English, and the notes also are interesting.... I think we should have some Gaelic matter in each number: there seems to be enough to do this, and overlaps will not matter if not both in the same number. I agree that "Going Home" seems to be especially good.... As we are at last beginning with Gaelic in earnest, I think the notes will make a good introduction. It would be good if we could get something new from S. Maclean. Thus we would be following on well from MacInnes's review of Macaulay's poems.

135

Alan Jackson, "Whip Whip Hooray." If I did suggest publishing this I think it would show I was agreeing out of fear of lack of liberalism, and that is a worse deprivation of freedom than my rejection of it would be. This seems to be a kind of phantasy that puts it in a class of poems I am down on, because they gratify the writer first and the reader is somehow expected to share in his gratification. D. H. Lawrence would have disapproved of this on grounds of its obscenity, and his way of approaching these things is still, I think, the best working method.

Donald John MacLeod, "Gaelic Culture." We need this sort of thing, and this article is vigorously expressed and I was interested in the information it gives. If it says anything that other Gaels would disagree with, they may write accordingly.

R. B. Watson, "Signatures." Too much like an exercise in amateur philosophising and educated idea-grubbing, to be marked with approval by a schoolmaster who knows it all himself.

Bernard Kodjo Laing, "Resurrection." Needs discussion. Worth printing whole if it can be done, but obvious difficulties here. Difficult poem only in detail. General effect and purpose clear enough.... It is an angry or even desperate protest of a man in the middle of a ring of frightening people. Is it one of the first-class poems of our time?

D. M. Black, "A Journey in Japan." You may be surprised, but this fascinates me and leaves me with a feeling of having been in a very foreign place. Perhaps his time there has made him unaware that this seems slight to us, and perhaps we should welcome this as a very Japanese piece. It also leaves me after one reading with a lot of bits of information about Japan, which may not be slight after all.

D. M. Black, "Peter MacCrae Attempts the Active Life." I think this was not sent as a possible contribution. If so, I am sorry to say

I am glad, for it bewilders me. But Sydney Tremayne nearly two years ago said how lucky we were to have D. M. Black as a contributor, and I thought so too, so intensely vigorous, positive, crystalline.

Derek Bowman, translation of Brecht poems. Yes, certainly let us choose from these. They are very good poems, and very well translated, so far as I can judge. They are MUCH better in English than almost anything we see here, written in English to start with, or in Scots, either.

9 March 70

D. M. Black, "Peter MacCrae Attempts the Active Life." I do not like the impropriety of this, and others may feel the same way, but as crit. this is beside the point, it could be argued. I agree it is a remarkable work.

24 March 70

Alasdair Gray, *Lanark*. This is extraordinary, sure enough, and becomes more so as it goes on. We must have some of it. What about the whole of Chapter Seven, perhaps? Or another chapter from near the end? It is certainly a find; we mustn't let it go.

24 August 70

Lorn Macintyre, "Lara." I would throw my weight about as a greybeard and as an editor and ask him to cut out large chunks of this, or else. No need to say which chunks, perhaps, but I mean all this "I am no longer..." stuff, all this commonplace social injustice detail and revolutionary cliché. It is very good in parts. I would not have the whole, even as a promise of better things to come.

9 November 72

Alan Jackson, poems. I also strongly advise that we accept these *in toto*, and give them a good spread of space. (He is one of the few poets, I think, who are blessed with negotiable mental anguish.)

137

Extracts from letters to Michael Schmidt

The correspondence between Robert Garioch and Michael Schmidt concerned first the compilation of *Made in Scotland*, edited by Robert Garioch and published in 1974 by Carcanet Press, and then the editing of a selection from Sir David Lindsay, the latter being completed but not published at the time of Garioch's death. Most of the correspondence is concerned with practical editorial matters, but I have extracted several passages of wider interest.

R. F.

16 Oct 72

Here is a new Belli translation No. 1723, still with the translator's sweat glistening on it: art is to conceal art, aw'rite, but sometimes anguished effort may show through and give a kind of aesthetic pleasure.

2 May 73

Here is my suggested list of 12 good men, perhaps subject to alteration. For this purpose I think it is a very good idea to exclude any who are in *The Oxford Book of Scottish Verse*, on the grounds that they must be comparatively well-known on that account. Tom Scott left himself out of that book, but I think he could be considered too well-known on other grounds. Paul Mills is the best of the young ones, I am pretty sure, but others are nearly as good, and I like the idea that more anthologies may follow, so they may be in the next. William Kay has the very good poem in Scots that won the Grierson Prize in Edinburgh University. It looks on Glencoe (the prescribed subject) from an Ayrshire covenanting point of view, very remarkable, and it is well-handled too. But I don't know what else he has written. He may be a genuine one-poem man, legitimately as represented in the anthology. The excellence of Duncan Glen's poetry is not evident to me, but perhaps it should be in, just the same. I think Donald Campbell should be in, but wonder if he has written enough good ones. Some of his are certainly good enough. I have a lot of respect for Forbes MacGregor's (the whale man's) poetry and it has been very little published. I hope he will be regarded as my discovery.

With him and W. Kay and D. Campbell we would have three/twelve in Scots, which is not a big percentage, but just about true to the facts as they are just now.

Rayne Mackinnon is very well qualified also, on grounds of quality and obscurity.

Enclosed are my three books that are not out of print (a sad double-negative).

11 May 73

Yes. I agree, we should have a glossary. I have learned from my mistake of not having one for *Jephtha*, owing to a puristic phase that caused me even to use the word *copyricht*.

I was very pleased to get Michael Hamburger's book. It is a fine collection with a quality of dignity about it, and an extraordinary range, and generosity of quantity. Sydney Tremayne in a letter told me he had bought it. He has long had a high opinion of Hamburger.

Also I am very pleased to have Christopher Smart. I have always read his poetry with reluctance, and have been fascinated by it when I did read it, and then become reluctant again, but I have never had a copy of my own. I am glad you put your cat on the cover in honour of his cat Jeoffry: a very good idea, and it does look well enlarged, with yellow eyes. For a long time I thought a carcanet was a cat, not expecting to find the word in a dictionary.

...criteria used to decide whether a poet is too famous for inclusion: (a) a book to himself from a big (London) publisher, (b) inclusion in *The Oxford Book of Scottish Verse*, (c) share in one of the Penguin Modern Poets books, (d) choice by Poetry Book Society....

You are right, I am not wealthy, I meant to agree, but forgot. I'm not broke, but have to be careful, and have a tendency to be niggardly anyhow.

17 May 73

Thank you for the four Pessoa translations, neat, in a case. I am pleased to get these. He seems to be much the sort of man I like to read, and the translations are fresh and good, so far as I can tell.

I should like to keep the anthology list I sent you as final. I do think we should include Duncan Glen. He has been absurdly praised in *Stand* by Anne Cluysenaar, who is a specialist in stylistics and ought to know.... But I think he should be included. I think I see how Pete Morgan's poems work, and think they often succeed.

Yes, we should explain the quadruple rule, and certainly say "Major Publisher." I forget that all in London is not big.

12 July 73

It would be good to have an essay on my work; I should think so, I mean, but I have almost nothing to submit, certainly nothing like a collection, which is vexing, when you make me this offer, which would have been the very thing I was waiting for, ten years ago, but the Lines Review Edition just out has used up all I had left, as I fear will be rather apparent, and I am infertile; in fact, a good many of my recent few deliveries have been no-balls, which I am sorry about, though I appreciate your offer very well. I must read more, and have in fact taken to Chaucer, which may be a good sign. Sydney Tremayne told me he has been reading Wordsworth: that seems a good idea also.

I am glad you are to have an interview with Edgell Rickwood.

I wonder if you could have an essay on Sydney Tremayne's work: it seems very good to me.

Some of your suggested discussions look like being very helpful to me. I am in a desperate state of puzzlement (or would be if I gave way to despair) because nothing in poetry, art, music etc seems to be too feeble-minded, ever.

6 Aug 73

I think all these figures are correct, but have only counted them once, not twice as I always had to do in the grim days of school registers and things (if they couldn't get their main totals to balance they always came to me first, and that was out of habit) — I mean in Bonnington Road School about 1933-34, because at a certain stage I was always right, even if I took all day to make certain, while all around me was left to chaos. Far more important to get your totals correct than to stop the big boys thumping the little girls, or vice versa all four ways. They had a primitive sort of intercom and the headmaster was always phoning me if anything was wrong with the savings-bank balance or whatnot, even after I had abandoned all else for the sake of accountancy. He kept his pointer always to my number. So I put a fault on my phone, behind the panel. It may be there yet.

9 Dec 73

Thank you for *Poetry Nation One*. I wonder if I sent a subscription for it; I shall do so, if not. This is a new kind of periodical, at least so far as I know, and it is a good idea to have a large critical section, not a review section, which is not the same thing. Certainly I agree with the tendency I see here to insist on poetry being a serious matter that takes a lot of doing, and to maintain it is not being a poet that matters but making poems. I should be glad to see an open and clear demonstration that the productions of a whole *quueae* of poets who are just not worth the paper they are printed on (less, in fact: I had forgotten that paper is now a lot scarcer than alleged poems, so that figure is now out of date). And this in spite of the fact that I am still on civil terms with a lot of dud poets, with or without guitars. And then there is this wearifu Marxism, a necessary orthodoxy for the daringly outspoken, who bow before so much polite applause at poetry-readings, and what a lot of little hairy ginsbergs there are, with their three-chord tricks, and those soppy girls smoothing down their amami hair over their wearifu microphones, intoning their sermons all to one text! I know a lot about this sort of thing, through waiting my turn to perform with what breath I can take of the smoke that passes for air, while those characters get through with what passes for poetry and music. It is all too easy, that's the trouble: at least the wee lassies who used to weary us at Sunday school concerts had taken a lot of trouble to play the piano as well as they did, even if it was pretty terrible to listen to.

19 Jan 74

Burns Singer's poetry I think as good as you think it is. I like that fertile kind of poetry. I met him once, long ago, at G. S. Fraser's in Chelsea. I liked him but found him alarmingly active. I suspect he could be a ruthless friend.

141

I am now muddled about expenses (one more thing to do, to keep a note and not lose it) but I can work it out, mainly so that I don't lose when they make deductions from my Old Age Pension. And, I've just thought, please don't pay me any money until after the end of September, when my Dictionary job ends. Meanwhile, the pay from that is just under the limit allowable to o.a. pensioners. One has to think of all these things.

Yes, it is a very presentable book, I think. The weak point, I suppose, is D. Campbell (and he thinks such a lot of himself too, Ah well). I think M. Reynolds is good in a quiet way. P. Mills is the best of the lot, but T. Buchan is a good kicker and F. MacGregor can deliver a startling bumper. And everybody likes Liz Lochhead.

I know it is a great thing to have one's *Collected Poems* published, but it does seem too soon, with one small selection so recently published and the other two still selling slowly. I think it would never do to publish poems that are still getting the publishers their money back. There is almost nothing that I have written that is not thus still in print, except *The Masque of Edinburgh*. This is a good offer and I appreciate it, but it does seem too soon for me to accept it. I do wish that the booksellers would expose for sale *The Big Music* and *Doktor Faust in Rose Street*. I think they would sell, if only they were to be found. But neither Caithness Books nor Macdonald has an outfit of commercial travellers. I have done a little of that myself, locally, but don't like doing it.

I am very pleased that the Carcanet Press, of which I think highly, should offer to publish my *Collected Poems*, only I was concerned about Macdonald and Caithness Books, and also there is the knowledge that I have almost nothing new. Carcanet is an acceptable outlet, all right. So I am very willing to make a firm acceptance of your offer to publish this book in 1977/8 or some such date; I should like to say first having consulted or at least informed the previous publishers, which I have not done.

I am allowed to earn £10 per week without losing my pension, now that I am no longer working with the *Dictionary of the Older Scottish Tongue*. Some finesse might be practised, i.e. if I am paid by anyone else I lose the pension for that week, so I can earn any amount more during that week without losing any more for that week. I suggest that when you are ready, you wait till I tell you someone has paid me for some odd job early in a week, and ask you to pay me before the Saturday ending that week, and then all will go in together as weekly earnings. That way I lose only one week's pension, which is inevitable. But the same result would be obtained if you were to send me not more than £10 per week for the necessary number of weeks.

22 Dec 74

Thank you for that big parcel of books "Credit against Royalty" (which sounds as if it might be the title of a book): a good selection, that I am glad to get. E. Morgan is very bright, is he not? It is good to find somebody so flexible who also has a sound academic stock of knowledge all immediately available and sorted out in his head. I was pleased to find that he had been placed in the van by Robin Fulton in that new book *Contemporary Scottish Poetry* (Macdonald). R. Fulton is another bright-brained man, much needed in our Scottish situation, which is short of proper criticism. . . .

I was hoping to send you a group of poems all about perception and optical illusions, but got into very heavy going and saw clearly that I had set about this in the wrong way and had somehow not noticed how bad the first two poems of the set were; though I had doubts I couldn't see that they were all wrong. This is disappointing, but I think the idea is worth another try.

13 Feb 75

I think I should not take on the job of writing about Burns Singer, not knowing enough about him. I do think he was a good poet, but that is a general memory of what I have thought; I can't remember anything about it, and it might take a lot of work for me to write this article, without the results being good enough.

Callum Macdonald has been saying for a month or three that he would like to publish my *Collected Poems* (which I have done nothing in the matter of collecting yet) and I should like him to do so, since he was my first and for a long time only publisher, and I hope you won't mind, since I think there was a chance that you might do them, and I didn't say no. Now last week, Reprographia has been asking me about this — I said Callum Macdonald should come first. Then he asked about the Belli translations, of which there are now about thirty-five, and I hope there may be more soon as I have found a new coach. The third lot of new things I have is thirty-one of what I call my pop-poems. I have been recording one per week since Radio Forth started. It is a commercial radio company. This is what some would call doggerel, though I doubt if that word has any meaning. Perhaps you might publish the sonnets and Reprographia the Radio Forth Rhymes or the other way round, or no way round. I take these pop-poems seriously, but they are poohpoohed by the knowledgeable of course.

Yes, I shall write to Callum Macdonald and ask him if he would produce the book under a joint imprint with Carcanet, which seems a good idea to me, but I don't know what he will think. My quandary is that you were first to suggest the possibility of a *Collected Poems*, and he was the first to publish them at all, when all but he had fled. And I would have to make up my mind whether the Belli should be both in the *Collected* and in a book to itself. And I want to wait, or am tempted to wait and see if I produce anything new, or if the *Collected* should have nothing new in it, which would make me ashamed, and show up my present barrenness. I even reflect uneasily that it should be called *The Complete Works*, perhaps. Meanwhile I am waiting for my prose book to be published "in November," but we shall see. I should like it to be before Christmas. I don't know about the rest of Scotland, but the Edinburgh bookshops are full of visitors just now, though of course many of them are Americans with the ten-bob dollars.

I have a lot of ill-assorted things to do just now: a course of lectures to prepare for some American Quakers, and some reading of Scottish novels I must do (I never read anything like enough, especially prose) for a Workers' Educational set of lectures, and there has to be something in pop fourteeners every Friday for Radio Forth (I have got very interested in this) and a man I like very much coming to stay with us next week. He is famous (among thaim that kens) for translating Hegel, whom I can't understand even in his much-approved translation, but must try again.

19 Oct 75

I am very pleased to hear from Callum Macdonald that he likes the idea of a joint publication of my *Collected Poems*, or what I am inclined to think of as *Complete Poetical Works*, since there is nothing much that is new, except that the Belli sonnet translations still go on, so that would at least be something new to offer the astonished world; now rather a lot of them, 38 in all, but Callum seems to view them without alarm. Maybe we should wait a while to see if I produce anything worthwhile on my own. In fact, in my capacity as Poet Laureate to Radio Forth, I turn out one poem of 28-30 fourteeners each week, last week's being No. 43, and some of these might be included for a lark, to delight the captious critics, or even to function as Leviathan's tub. There have just appeared the first few copies of my prose work: *Two Men and a Blanket* (Southside), 183pp, £4.50, which price frightens me, but it is a very pleasing production, printed by Constable, I'm delighted to say. Mrs J. H. Caird (Janet Caird) asked me to read her collection of 34 poems and to suggest who might publish it. (She is already much published here AND IN AMERICA as a popular novelist and short-story writer, but that's a different matter.) Well, I said I had to write to you in any case, and would ask you about this. They are all one-page poems, and add up to a really fine and gloomy collection on the theme of human dissolution, with no perceptible sign of Christian hope (or any other) to weaken the effect....

7 June 79

I intend to ask Forbes Macgregor for a copy of *The Gowks of Mowdieknowes* to send you. I have not seen him for several months, but that is just as it has happened. He is going strong, I hear, and his book of Scots proverbs is selling by the 1,000; so Jimmie Annand told me recently. Also his book of jokes, *Macgregor's Mixture*, is to be seen in many shops. The title is allusive to Dr. Gregory's Mixture, an awful cathartic medicine they used to give to children, especially in Scotland, and especially in Edinburgh, I think, scene of the late Dr. Gregory's labours. In Glasgow, I think, parents favoured "yle," rather; the stuff they put in Castrol R, etc. So many engineers in Glasgow, of course. Nowadays children's bowels seem to move of their own accord. There used to be (still is?) a psalm or paraphrase sung in kirks with the line, "To thee, to all, my bowels move."

I really am interested in the Sir David Lyndsay, if you think it is a good idea.

13 June 79

I should tell you more about Callum Macdonald, whose publishing you might not understand, about his exploitation of the market, since he was the first (at Sydney Goodsir Smith's urgent urging) to publish my *Selected*, and, fact, years before (at the same urging) he published my *Masque of Edinburgh*. And it may be that selling Scottish books in Scotland is like selling breeks to Heilanmen. And Callum, we know, is a heilanman himself. He came out alive from Bomber Command (one of the few) with some money and started a printing firm with an Adana (one of the vertical kind, not like my flat-bed) and by degrees has now got a big printing works and out of his goodness has become Macdonald Publishers. So you will see how I respect him as the first publisher of my verse and also the most recent (the prose-book, which must have sold best, was published by Canongate-Southside). So if you can amicably become an aider and abettor of his good work, that will be very good.

4 July 79

...Yesterday I produced a translation of a Belli sonnet, guaranteed true to Belli's rhyme-scheme in this case. Here is a copy, of which I am as proud as a cat fetching a mouse into the drawing-room of a barren block of concrete flats.

146

My address has somehow got on to your books as Nelson Place—NOT SO: it is Street. One of the two recent letters was returned "not known," but got here at the second time of asking. The "Place" is only 50 yards away, a short street with a mews at the end of it. We don't know one another here: it is the only thing I don't like about the New Town, apart from dry-rot and near-18th-century drain pipes and rusty gas mains (yesterday I saw one they had just taken up in Northumberland Street; oh!). We are nice enough people, as far as I know, but don't meet much, except in emergencies. The people I always wave to are a Polish family, and a young French wife whose parents live in the Boulevard St. Michel. (I am a bit over-reserved myself, certainly.)

One good thing is that I don't want any royalties, at least not before you have cleared the costs. This is quite business-like on my part, as the money I get from poetry mostly comes from readings and magazines and so on, so it pays me if my poems become better known as a result of your publishing and in fact I am grateful. Besides, of course, I like people to read them.

It gives me great pleasure to see your enthusiasm, especially as I am become such a dry stick that I am ashamed.

Meanwhile I shall get on with the glossary, a soothing sort of job involving a lot of neat bits of paper....

No notes? I feel guilty about this, but if we have notes at all there will have to be a lot of them and take up too much room. I suggest that we recommend that readers who wish very full information will find any amount of it in Hamer's edition.

I met Michael Hamburger, yesterday evening, guest of Derek Bowman, of the Dept. of German here. He gave a reading. I very much like that man, and feel impressed by his poetry. And he speaks warmly of Carcanet.

Letters to Antonia Stott

30 April 75

I asked Mr Derek Bowman if he could suggest someone who might help me to translate some of the Belli sonnets. He suggested that I should ask you, and now I am taking the liberty of doing so.

Enclosed are some samples translated, with the texts and notes I sent to Miss Carla Spadavecchia, whom I met when she was a student in Edinburgh. Now she has gone home to Milan. The texts are from the Feltrinelli edition. The notes are in two parts, first, those by Belli, with additions in square brackets by the editor. The second set, referred to by line numbers, are by the editor. Their general purpose is to explain Romanesco words to Italian readers. Miss Spadavecchia gave me a literal translation in English, which I then tried to translate, and in some cases failed.

I can only just manage to read Italian with the help of a dictionary, and with the notes, which give the Italian equivalents of Romanesco words. But if I have a literal translation I can see quite well where the meanings come from, so I'm not translating from the translation. So if you would help me by providing literal translations I should be very grateful indeed. I enclose Nos. 1871, 1872, 2023 and 1861, which I sent to Miss Spadavecchia's address, but as she had gone to Italy they were returned to me, and have been in the drawer all this time.

It is difficult for me to pick out those sonnets that seem likely to serve my purpose, and sometimes I make a mistake and choose one that I can do nothing with, but that does not happen often....

It may be that you are busy, and can't do this—if so that is understood, but if you can help me I shall be very pleased.

P.S. I remember the good work you used to do for *Scottish International*.

Here are five of the sonnets you translated for me, all of them very well worth doing. No. 358 has a good example of the BAD luck that sometimes attends Scots: *dead*, *head* and *bed* all rhyme, but not *deid*, *heid* and bed. (But the luck often goes the other way.) When this happens I just honestly admit defeat and put it down as it is.

No need of a reply to this. You will certainly be busy and otherwise engaged for the rest of the summer. There are still some left for me to do.

This is a big help. I am very grateful.

Note: the MS date of No. 358 is 22 June 75.

15 December 75

Thank you for these two sonnets, which are both good ones, especially, I think, "La famija poverella," very moving. I have not translated the others you sent; "Ricciotto de la Ritonna" especially is a fine bit of one-sided flyting. It vexes me to get so little done of what I want to do. And I am supposed to be retired!

Here is a copy of my book, a small return.

They are going to publish "The Phisolopher Café Proprietor" in the periodical of the Association for Scottish Literary Studies, with the Italian, as I asked them to.

Please translate for me some day No. 2125, "Li cardinali in cappella." I think we should not have too many of these anti-clerical ones, which are more removed from our life, but that one is easily understood here also.

Note: "La famija poverella," "The Puir Faimly," is No. 1677.
    "Ricciotto de la Ritonna," "Dick of the Rotunda Mairket," is No. 1472.
    "The Phisolopher Café Proprietor" is No. 805.

6 January 76

Thank you for this, so good that I did it at once, and a great struggle it was, not too evident I hope. One trouble was that I started off with a set of rhymes too difficult, if not impossible. I doubt if the words exist —

There's forty-echt: I countit them masel:
yin of them white, and forty-seiven reid.

Ah well, I should ken better.

Note: this refers to No. 2125, "Cardinals in Chapel." The first stanza of the final
version is:

> I countit them mysel: there's echt-and-forty:
> yin of them white, the ither forty-sevin
> reid, chummlin the sairvice up til Hevin,
> set in their stalls, some buirdlie, some gey tottery.

18 March 76

I have been very slow, but here at last are these two, both done
yesterday. I have tried to do these before and failed. The word
swelt (= die) came to my aid, by the grace of God. I am relieved
when I find that a sestet rhymes *cdcede*. I wonder if we could find
some more religious, but not anti-clerical sonnets, to balance things
a bit. These two are very good, that you sent, away back in
October. Macdonald is setting up a *Collected Poems* for me, and as
I have little new these days, the point of new interest may be the
Belli translations, 43 so far, counting yesterday's two. Meanwhile it
seems best not to do any later than 2140, "The New Pope," which is
a good one to end a selection.

Please tell me some day if all nouns with final -e are plural. 1818,
"Le gabbelle" means "The Taxes," sure enough, but I am not sure
that 1272, "Le maledizzione" can mean "The Curses," since it seems
to make better sense in the singular.

Thank you, anyhow: I must get a move on.

Note: In Notebook Four the two Belli sonnets dated 17.3.76 are "The Relicshaw"
(No. 811) and "Immoral Reflections in the Coliseum" (No. 1619).

12 May 76

I must say your dramatisation of Belli is astonishingly good; I
never could see how you were going to set about it, but you have
seized the dramatic possibilities wonderfully, I think. It should be
very theatrical to look at as well as to hear, and the stage setting
simple enough too. I see it as a pageant with spoken words,
somewhat on the lines of Orff's *Carmina Burana*, only it has music
and not speech.

It is a very good idea to run two sonnets together as in the beginning, etc. I'm delighted to find that the verse becomes dialogue so easily, but would not have expected it to go quite as well as that.

That is a good choice of sonnets too, and they all do what the title promises; really, I'm most taken with this. We might approach the TV. I don't know who runs the drama in the BBC or ITV, but we could soon find out.

I've made some changes in the text, improvements, I hope. PTO for really improved version of "Judgment Day." I never was happy about the darkie and the lichtie, quite apart from being scared of the Race Relations Act: we are used to associating darkies with cotton-picking. Also there was a doubtful translation, now corrected, I hope. Carne-Ross was never sure, I remember, away back in 1958 I think it must have been, about what he thought was some sort of bell-collar, in connection with the angels.

JUDGMENT DAY

Fowre muckle angels wi their trumpets, stalkin
til the fowre airts, sall aipen the inspection;
they'll gie a blaw, and bawl, ilk to his section,
in their huge voices: "Come, aa yese, be wauken."

Syne sall crawl furth a ragment, a haill cleckin
of skeletons yerkt out fir resurrection
to tak again their ain human complexion,
like choukies gaitheran roun a hen that's clockan.

And thon hen sall be Gode the blissit Faither;
he'll pairt the indwellars of mirk and licht,
tane doun the cellar, to the ruiff the tither.

Last sall come angels, swarms of them, in flicht,
and, like us gaean to bed without a swither,
they will blaw out the caunnles, and guid-nicht.

I hope it is better now. Also, the first line of "The Mowdert Spinster" is now

It's nae guid speiran at me, Maistress Cant

(CANT, quite a common name in Scotland) The trouble was that *to speir* is an intransitive verb, usually followed by *at*.

I'm impressed by your handling of Scots. What a good idea to show the priest teaching his Latin! Very dramatic that should be. Also the scene with the advocate. A good idea to make the café proprietor a kind of chorus.

Enclosed is a new translation, quite successful and a good choice. I must get on with it. I'm inexplicably sweirt, but all right when I get started. There are now 41 in proof for the *Collected*, and I have sent 3 more, and this afternoon's one will make another.

In "The Mowdert Spinster" I've changed *shit* to *dirt*, thinking the word too strong for the context in Scots, though maybe less so in Romanesco. *Dirt* has a literary history, too, in Scots, e.g. much used by Lewis Grassic Gibbon. Please tell me some time what you think.

Also, in No. 272, last line, I have succumbed to temptation and translated "buggiarà sto Governo si se serva" as "the Government is buggert, oniegait." Please tell me some time if the word could correctly be thus translated, or if it is just an accidental resemblance. The sense is right anyway, and the translator is likely to grab it in recompense for losing an allusion, as in this new one, the "Poor Christian." That's delightful!

P.S. The reason why I asked you about the -e singular especially in connection with "Le maledizzione," No. 1272, was that I had translated this one before, with the help of Carla Spadavecchia (and I hadn't realised before that *sword* and *spade* started as the same word) who translated it as "The Curse," and there was a time after she had gone home to Milan that I took it in my head it must be plural. Now that point is cleared up, at least. When your translation arrived, I compared it with the Scots and found I had missed a nice point in l.11, where Belli implies we are not very big, but grubs are even smaller. So I wonder if this new version of lines 9-11 would be better, not so neat, but more accurate: what does an honest translator do?

THE CURSE

Our Monseigneur, his missal in his neive,
wi fowre screichs and twa shaks of halie-water,
has gane to curse the reivan Clan Gresshopper
out of the corn, forbidding them to thieve.

To caa this ban, that winnae gie them leave
tae eat, nae Christian act, wad be improper,
and yet it seems to me owre big a whopper
fir even ma smaa judgment to believe.

The gresshopper, cockroach and caiterpillar
are aa Gode's bairns, ay, an sae are we,
binna, tho we're no big, they're even smaller.

Hou is it, think ye, that Monseigneur Crucifer
may curse them, and syne preach to you and me
that it is sinfu, even to curse Lucifer?

Lines 9-11 as previously:

Gresshoppers, caiterpillars, grubs, are aa
Gode's craiturs, and sae, jist the same, are we,
binna that we are big and they are smaa.

I am tempted to call a *gresshopper* a *girsshopper*, but I won't! I wonder if that word was ever used? Must look up the S.N.D.

It will be good to have the other *Curse* poem that you sent, to keep this one company. There is a note in my edition that says that this idea of letting-up on the Deil is in *Tristram Shandy*. Fancy that! It is just the sort of thing Belli might think of, and Sterne too.

No. 1266 — I have changed *christening* to *kirsnin* — genuine Scots usage, by metathesis, I think they call it (like *gress-girss*).

All these changes are in aid of this *Collected*, to try and get it right, once for all (supposing such a thing possible). It is a blessing that Callum Macdonald is quite unusually patient in tholing alterations at the galley stage. Ordinary printers charge extra, so much that authors, I believe, often have to go without their afterthought-improvements because they would cost too much. I hope you can use these that I suggested without upsetting your text too much.

I wonder if you could produce this play at the University, and after that, we shall see. Perhaps you could offer it to the Traverse or somewhere as a complete production. I don't know, I am quite ignorant of theatrical affairs. But I can imagine this as being very effective. Quite remarkable.

Note: The play referred to here is Antonia Stott's dramatisation of some of the sonnets.

The offending l.10 of No. 273 was:

He'll wale them out, the darkie(s) frae the lichtie(s),

"The Mowdert Spinster" is No. 1640.

"this afternoon's one": "The Curse" No. 1585 is dated 12.5.76 in MS, and this is "the other curse poem" referred to later in the letter.

No. 272 is "That's Waur."

The allusion at the end of the letter to the "poor christian" is to No. 1585, l.11.

20 May 76

Here are three more sonnets, all worth doing. Yes, I always want more, though sometimes I'm a long time about using the ones I have. I think these are now all you have sent me, except for one which I had to give up for lack of rhymes and inability to avoid necessary words. Please have a look at No. 1662, which is like No. 1677. I think we have enough anticlerical ones to be going on with, and should look at some others, especially the social ones, i.e. especially those that are mainly fun. I am much taken with "La fin der monno." Do you know what that hole is like, near St. Paul's? Whatever can it be? The one, I mean, that the Nochelia is to come out of. I should like to go and see it some day, if it's still there. That sonnet seems a good mixture of theology and popular notions.

Good luck also to your play: it looks very promising to me.

P.S. St. Paul's Bunk — a far-fetched translation, I admit. But there is the expression "bunkie-hole," a place for children to hide in. Such are the resources of Scots!

Note: "three more" — judging by MS dates there could be four to choose from: No. 873 (13 May), No. 799 (14 May) and Nos. 1677 and 274 (15 May).

No. 1622 is "The Guid-Hertit Aunt"

No. 1677 is "The Puir Faimly"

"La fin der Monno," "The Warld's End," is No. 274, and includes the reference to "St. Paul's Bunk."

1 June 76

Here are the three sonnets, for which many thanks. Some of these have pretty frantic rhyming, I fear, but that is part of the fun, I hope. I was glad to have No. 1662 to match that other one, and I like these ones about his adventures in the streets, well, I don't know if there are many of these, but I think there is one in which somebody goes for him with a knife, and he acquits himself rather well. That is a good one about the King, and one that would probably be expected, being well-known. I spelt Nochelia in a Scottish way, and was about to change it, but decided not to do so. What a strange story! I did not understand that the hole was a cave in a rock. I thought of a hole in the street!

The bells in "The Day of Judgment" — Donald Carne-Ross was thinking of some word that means a bell-collar for a horse or something, but I remember he said he was doubtful. I'm glad that has been put right after nearly twenty years.

My wife or I or both of us are mostly at home, but not always, of course, so a ring from your husband would make sure. 556-1732.

There are now about 51 Belli sonnets, perhaps enough for the *Collected Poems*, but I should like to go on indefinitely as long as you care to furnish me with cribs: it is frantic kind of fun, and keeps my hand in, now that my invention is showing signs of wear. Also I think the Carcanet Press will still be interested in a small bookful. I must write to them. It is one of the things I forget to do. They want to pay me money, too, for that anthology.

It is a good job you told me you are on leave: I hope I have not troubled the University. Yes, when the time comes I shall write to the BBC etc. I have no influence there, but at least some of them know who I am.

P.S. I'm glad you point out the *voi* & *lei* in 1662. I have done my best with it. Scots speakers do often say *you* when they are being abusive. I guess that *lei* similarly is more "correct."

Note: this letter is unsigned, or perhaps a third page is lost. The anthology referred to is presumably *Made in Scotland* (Carcanet, 1974), edited by G.

Lei is a formal and colder address than *voi* (which G. rendered as *ye* in No. 1662).

19 May 77

Here is my book, which I am delighted to give you, especially as you helped so much with the Belli part of it. I should like to try some more of the sonnets you have translated for me, and then we shall see, but meantime I need a rest, for fear of becoming jaded. But we shall see.

The book arrived for me this morning to review. ABBA, by

Anthony Burgess (Faber). The idea is that Belli and Keats have met, and sixty or seventy translations are the outcome. Very good translations, too, in rhyme, the language I suspect more sweary than the original. Of course I'm only partly qualified to write this review, not knowing how vulgar some of his words were, but I suspect that in this trans. they have been made more so.

However, I've only had a quick look this morning.

I'm pleased to see some more interest in Belli. Translating him might become "all the rage," a fashionable cult, or such like.

Anyhow, it gives me pleasure to give you this book, which is your due.

Note: the book is, of course, the *Collected Poems* of 1977.

2 Jan 78

Thank you for your Christmas card, very beautiful, the curve of that brow, and all, a marvel, really.

It seemed the only possible thing to send you in return would be a Belli translation, and here, D. G. (I mean it!) is one nearly up to standard, only I had to make it *aabb*, you can see why. But I'm pleased to have managed to do it at all after a long time of laziness that encouraged a fear that I couldn't do it any more. So I am pleased both with your card and with my jobby accomplist.

A happy new year to you and to your man, as the old folk would put it in Scotland.

P.S. A note in the Feltrinelli edition says *Nostro Signore: il papa,* so I've followed it.

I noticed in the well-performed play on ITV last night, *Saturday, Sunday, Monday,* translated from Eduardo de Filippo, the distracted Neapolitans said something like CHOCH!

Note: the sonnet accompanying this letter was No. 1459, "The Thunner Yestreen."

6 July 79

I suddenly came to on Thursday and fetched out your literal translations, and here are three of them made into tolerable sonnets, which cheers me up greatly, one per day, and not bad either. The most recent previous one is dated Jan. 78, and the one before that June 76. I am sorry to have been so torpid, not encouraging for you, either, but I do appreciate your help. With a crib, I manage very well to read Belli, I mean, the meanings of the words are clear, and also the constructions of the sentences, but I don't know enough to make a translation by myself without great difficulty and a risk of howlers. I get the gist of "L'oro di Napoli," however; I am slow, but it is worth the trouble, well worth it. There are still two cribs unused.

It makes things easier for me when Belli rhymes the sestet *cdc*, *ede*. I am grateful to you for choosing the enclosed three of that kind.

Maybe Belli found it easier too, but he can't have had such difficulties in finding rhymes. Someone once told me that it is difficult in Italian to avoid rhymes where they are not wanted.

I don't see much point in translating sonnets without trying to rhyme them according to the original scheme (like Harold Norse) or by altering the sense (like Anthony Burgess). But it is a mercy to find the original has taken an easier way for once or twice.

Note: in the MS "Beauty" (No. 1338) is dated 29.6.76, and "The Thunner Yestreen" (No. 1459) is dated 2.1.78.

   L'oro di Napoli is a book of stories by Giuseppe Marotta which A. S. had given to G.

21 Sept 79

Here are four of your sonnets, many thanks to you. There is a fifth of that set, "La golaccia," which I seem to remember giving to somebody to publish in some magazine, but there is no note of it, and maybe that memory is all wrong. These are all well-chosen, and have come off well. They are easier for me if the sestet rhymes *cdc*, *ede*: you will readily understand why. I would very much like some more, if that isn't asking too much. Thank you for your post-card of Westminster Abbey lit up. That pleased me greatly. I wonder, what about No. 163, "The Wimshurst Machine," it seems to be? It has the *cdc*, *dcd*, but it can't be helped. There is a whole list of *casi curiosi*: I wonder about—156-7, 1134, 1181, 1363, 1373, 1954, 2050.

I wish I could read them with any sort of facility, but I can't.

I don't know if that is much of a list: I don't pretend that I am not helpless on my own; and that almost even goes for French, for my acquisition of which I have a Higher Leaving Certificate. Oh Lord! We called it the Highers to distinguish it from the Lower Leavings, or Dog's Breakfast.

I just remembered something I wanted to ask you, about a footnote to the Penguin translation of *La Chartreuse de Parme*, by M. R. B. Shaw (p. 129). "In Italy young men who have patrons or possess good intelligence become *Monsignori* or *prelati*, which does not mean bishop: they then wear purple stockings. A man does not take any vows to become *Monsignore*; he can discard his purple stockings and get married."

Really, I am concerned about my turning Belli's *Monsignore* into *Monseigneur*, which we British regard as near-English. I wish I had made it *Monsignor*.

All this astonishes me. Belli seems to suggest (Nos. 1272, 2125, etc) that a monsignor is pretty well committed on his way to becoming a cardinal.

Note: "La golaccia," "Greed," is No. 1339. No. 163 was not translated.

7 Nov 79

Thank you for these three good cribs of good sonnets. Here is one ready, I think: this had me struggling, not too obviously I hope, in the end. Had to change the second bit to *baab*. Can't be helped. Your translation of the name of the unfortunate gentleman looks like a flash of genius. I don't know enough about *caccia* and *matti* to know how you worked it out, but willingly take your word for it. It is a powerful sonnet, very sad, though Patacchino's friend thinks it all a huge joke. There seem to be complicated allusions about Patacca, according to the notes in my edition, but I couldn't understand them, and just called him Harry. And in desperation I invented a place called Kilmore, having made as sure as I can from my gazetteer that there is no such place. If it's bad Gaelic I can't help it, either. Don't want to go bonkers over it.

Note: the sonnet referred to here and in the next letter is No. 156, "Gyte Again — I," and the second of the pair then mentioned in the next letter is No. 157, "Gyte Again — II."

158

Attempting the second of this pair, I realised what a mess I had made of lines 9 and 11 of No. 1, so here is a better version. Maybe Greasybeard will do in this sonnet of funny names, and a little bit in keeping with that puzzling note: "Patacco è sinon. del sesso fem., ma è anche, comme nella lingua, la macchia d'unto." Pity I couldn't make it Greasy Joan to get the gender right...could be done, maybe, and get a better rhyme for Laird? We'll see.

Weill, oniewey, much thanks!

Note: "Gyte Again—I," ll.9-11 in first version:

> Weill oniewey! Ye mind it fine, eh Harry,
> hou lang his harns hae been pleyin hy-jinks
> sen yon time whan he yuistae hurl a barrie?

Then in final version:

> Weill oniewey! ye'll mind, eh Greasybeard,
> hou lang his harns hae been pleyin hy-jinks
> ivver sen he wes coachman til the Laird.

With reference to the quotation, A. S. notes that G. misquoted here. It should read: "*Patacchino:* sopran. *Patacca* è sinon. del sesso femminile, ma è anche, comme nella lingua, la macchia d'unto." *Patacca* means grease stain and also has the extended meaning of female sexual organ, or, simply, woman.

I was too hasty in sending the first attempt at this one No. 1363, "The Customs Post," and next morning I realised that it wouldn't do. This is better, I hope.

Also there is difficulty with the very improper names in No. 156. I see now that "Greasybeard" is feeble and ridiculous and pointless. Maybe "Crumpetwilard?" I see in the cookery book that muffins are made with butter, so perhaps lard would do. I wonder if I am daft to try to get indecent double-meanings from one language into another. Still, if I am trying to cook, I may as well try to make a proper job of it.

There is still one for me to try to translate: No. 1373, rather a comical one that you sent me.

I do appreciate your help, especially as you have plenty to do already, and especially as I do these things by fits and starts.

P.S. I'll send this to an Aberdeen University magazine called *Open Space*. The editor has been asking for something and I hadn't anything left.

The West Port used to be one of the Edinburgh city-gates, and the Town Council did sometimes impose customs-duties. Arnott (18th cent.) piously remarks in his History that when the town mills were swept away in a flood by the Water of Leith, it was God's judgment on the Town Council for their wicked tax upon beer coming into Edinburgh.

Note: the version of No. 1363 accompanying this letter was the version as printed. No. 1373 does not seem to have been done.

23 Dec 79

Thank you for your Christmas card, a specially interesting one that I look at often.

I wanted to send you a Christmas sonnet, but found that even Belli was inclined to leave off at that time, but here is his very last one that I have tried to translate all on my own, at the risk of making howlers. I suppose this Regno di Napoli was what Garibaldi rose against: I don't know much about it.

Anyhow, here is this not-very-festive sonnet, with greetings for all that—

P.S. I have heard about those pipers that came in from the country. Maybe the cholera had stopped them. Belli seems to have been in an inn Ginggola in Trastavere, or pretended that these thirty-four sonnets were from there—I can't read the note with any accuracy, I think.

I like B.'s listing freethinking among all those calamities.

THE CHOLERA MORBUS

—Bit whit wanchancy times are ours! We hae
want and freethinking, weir, the pest, the rain,
spates, fludes, Britain and France and Spain,
aa faain in our times, my Agatha.

Richt nou, thir's cam upon us mickle adae
wi nestie seiknesses and stouns of pain
wrocht on us by the Neapolitan Reign,
waur than puir Punchinello suffert frae.

160

Still, Punch has tholit nae calamity
like Christ's, duin out of his nine days and nichts
of Novenas for his Nativitie.

This is the first Nativitie he saw
plenishit wi manger and the altar-lichts
without the pipers giean him a blaw.

Giuseppe Belli No. 2279, *Er Còllera mòribus* 24 dicembre 1836.

For Dr Antonia Stott, in gratitude for much help.

Robert Garioch, 23 December 1979.

Note: the final printed version goes:

> —Bit whit wanchancy times are ours! We hae
> freedom, fludes and weir, the pest, the rain
> that nivver gies owre, England, France and Spain,
> aa faain in our times, my Agatha.
>
> Richt nou, there's cam upon us mickle wae,
> this grugous nestie seikness that has gane
> through the distressfu Kingdom, and has taen
> yon puir Punchinello yesterday.
>
> Hard luck on Punch, bit nae calamity
> compared wi Jesus Christ's, duin out o's richts,
> nae novena for his Nativity.
>
> This is the first Christmas we ivver saw
> without a hope of cribs or altar-lichts
> and nut wan piper here to gie a blaw.

8 Jan 80

Thank you for the two translations. Yes, I had got things pretty far wrong with the two Christmassy sonnets, and it is good you were so patient about them. Still, they were well meant. But I shall let that be a lesson to me, very useful, and that is to keep the grammar-book in action (I have one) as well as the dictionary. I should have known that *era* is past tense, for instance. The word *libberta* in 2279 I took to mean *freethinking*, and so maybe it does, but it has a better effect to write *freedom* (not so obvious?). I was quite far astray with *Regno*, thinking that it was being blamed for the troubles (blame the Government!).

But it was in the Adam sonnet that I got the meaning all wrong. I shall have a go at sorting that one out also with the help of your crib.

L   161

No need to answer this. I don't want to be always bothering you in the midst of your own concerns. But I am greatly obliged all the same.

P.S. Not content with 1.8 of 2279, but maybe the best I can do. Might find another place-name?

Note: No. 2279 1.8 exists in an earlier version as —

> yon puir wee Punchinello of Cerra

The "Adam" sonnet does not seem to have been translated.

24 March 80

Sonnet 1339 is on page 70, thanks to you, without whom, etc. I really am very grateful for your help. It is good to show what Belli could do with a sad truth that everybody knows already. *Auld-faither* means *Grandfather*.

I have not done any sonnets lately, being obsessed with a Selection and Introduction etc to Sir David Lindsay. I've been making heavy weather of it, but it is nearly ready, and should be pretty good, I hope. It is for the Carcanet Press. I keep changing my mind, and doing bits over again.

No need to answer this: I don't want to bother you.

Note: The p. 70 refers to *PN Review*, VI:6, in which No. 1339 was published.

25 Nov 80

Here are three translations done with your help: 1134, 1954 and 2050, also 1981, which is aided by a crib sent me by Alastair Mackie, who found it somewhere (I'd better find out about this). I hope it doesn't break too many rules to make a word *Inglesa* so as to rhyme with *Teresa*. In fact, this rhyming is a desperate business, and there is a disheartening time when one is trying to lay out a set of rhymes for the two parts of a sonnet, and awful moments when one realises that two "rhymes" are the very same word. Not much to do with poetry maybe, but I can't help that. I've done seventy of these sonnets to date.

There seems to be some interest in these translations just now. I read a review of an Oxford Book of Translations in which some of

162

these translations of ours (I think) appeared — the first I had heard of it, or else I have forgotten being asked, which is not unlikely, or being paid, which is less unlikely....

Now I think I have used all the cribs that you so kindly sent me, so I now sit up and beg for more. I have a list you sent me of recommended sonnets, and have ticked those done.

I cannot ever express sufficiently my gratitude for your help, without which, etc.

Note: the list contains nineteen numbers, all translated except No. 1603. Both Nos. 805 and 1677 are described as "specially good."

6 Dec 80

I am very grateful to you for sending so promptly these two translations of 279 and 67, and grateful also to the Muse for the rendering (or bashing) into sonnet form that is on the back of this sheet. It pleases me also that you like the three I sent you: they seem pretty good to me, and I have sent them to Michael Schmidt and he wrote saying he would print them in the *PN Review*, which is good, as it gives them an airing furth of Scotland, just when some notice is being taken of the sonnets in the Oxford Book....

I knew you had retired (Derek Bowman told me) but not that you had not been well. I am sorry about that. But I have found for my part how good it is to be retired. If I can keep up my end of this Belli industry, there may be something! At least he has plenty left.

P.S. Pity to abandon Belli's really masterful pun. Can't be helped. But the Aberdeen folk have these delightful double diminutives, e.g. *lass, lassie, lassockie.*

I think I shall use the upper alternative in the first line, an afterthought.

I'm not sure of the theology of my 7th line as a way round my inability to get in the word *excommunicate.* But it has always seemed to me that keeping somebody out of the church amounts to something like this. I remember an old man in Wester Ross very sad because his Free Presbyterian (I think) minister had banned him from the kirk for a period of weeks because he was not sober when the minister paid him a visit.

A *toorie,* or *tappietoorie,* is really a *tuft (panache),* but has come

163

to mean, somewhat loosely, any daft-looking object worn on the head. *Hiz* and *us* are the same word. *Firtae, for to* (very bad grammar in primary schools).

If you find a sonnet to contrast with 279, showing the Pope (Pio IX, more likely) in a more favourable way, we may have a nice pair of sonnets to send to some editor; I wonder if there are any more like 2140. What about the sonnets 2149 and following? 2149 itself seems ironical to me (people won't believe that I can't read these sonnets by myself, except dimly — with the help of a crib and a dictionary I can see how all the words fit together, but can't manage properly on my own) and it would be good if one could find one that makes a better contrast, if there is such a thing in this vast collection — maybe not.

Note: Garioch's P.P.S.'s are not always set out as such: his afterthoughts tend to crowd into odd corners of the pages. This letter had five such afterthoughts.

The versions of No. 279, "The Paip," which is included in this letter is the version printed. The deleted first line (as distinct from "the upper alternative," which was printed) is:

Gode wants a virgin Paip, for fear he'd mak

With reference to "the sonnets 2149 and following," Garioch did in fact translate Nos. 2149, 2150, 2151, 2152, 2153 and 2162.

13 Dec 80

Many thanks for the translations, arrived this morning, powerful poems they are too. I had got an over simple impression of Belli's having been keen on Pope Pio as a change from Gregory.

Here is the previous set, hope you like them.

Must hurry catch post.

16 Dec 80

Your last plentiful lot of first-rate cribs made me rise up and call you blessed. Sometimes your lines manage to become mine of their own accord, in places one bit of easement is that Belli at this late stage so often used *cdc, ede* in the sestet. Maybe he found it helped him to be more easy-going, even in Italian. I was most interested to see how much he likes Pope Pio, though his mildness makes him think better of Gregory's roughness. It does show the impossible position of a head of the church who is also the tyrant of a state, especially one where there is so much economic and social misery. I am, and long have been, impressed by that early expression, "Constantine's fatal gift." That series on the Good Pope is a remarkable character-study: I admire Belli more as I know him slightly better. In 2153 I have followed the Feltrinelli improper suggestion about the meaning of *Zebbedei*, which strikes even me, knowing nothing much, as an extraordinary word, "sinonimo di *coglioni*." I was irresistibly attracted in the first place, by the rhyme with *cardinals*; such gifts of fortune should not be lightly rejected. But, unless I have mistaken the tone of the sonnet, this is a marvellous performance, starting with rather pointless vulgarity and finishing very seriously and piously. I wonder if he started this very serious sonnet in this way so as to arouse the interest of a rough audience in a café? It has an artistic effect, all the same.

Both your edition and mine seem to have a full-stop wrongly placed in 2149, at the end of the eleventh line. Anyhow, I've moved it one line further on.

Please send 2152 and 418, when it suits you. I hope you don't mind my always asking for more.

I can't guarantee to keep things up, but am delighted as well as surprised by the liveliness of last week. It cheers me up especially as I have been so dull lately in the matter of any sort of writing.

P.S. We may as well take advantage of the Glasgow habit of putting *but* at the end.

Note: the P.S. refers to No. 535, l.7.

9 Jan 81

Here are the latest two, also 2143, revised. I am embarrassed about the first attempt at this one. I had misunderstood its attitude completely, thinking it was full of irony. Even the first line would never do at all. *Couthie*, I think, is just about the right word, still having something about it almost too gentle, but still not a cynical word. And an awful mistake I had made in line 8, thinking it had something to do with "turning the stomach" and reminding me of the scene in *Weir of Hermiston* with the father using that word to tell his son what he thinks of his delicacy in court. All wrong! I'm glad you put me right. In 2152 I looked up *salacca* and found *pilchard*, so I thankfully called him *Mr Spratt*, a much-needed rhyme. In 280 *staig-cheils* I found for *stable-boys* etc. It seems all right to spell *baldachin* thus in English. It must have been a strange construction. I couldn't improve on your "bluidie noble guairdsmen"—no need. I hope you like those. I thought the originals were specially good ones. Many thanks. Further contributions thankfully received. Just as experiment, I have tried hard to do a few by myself, and failed completely, though I can follow the words easily with your cribs. I mean, I see how all the words fit together, though on my own, with dictionary and grammar-book, I give up.

P.S. Please do away with that first copy of 2143, or alter the offending parts, at least.

Yes: in 2149 I see the full-stop is right enough, I've changed it.

I sent all the recent ones to Michael Schmidt just because he is interested and hope he will put some (not all, of course) into *PN Review*.

Note: No. 2143 is "The Easy-gaun Paip." The original first line ended with "...sweetie-hairt!" (presumably thought of at first as ironical) and the "awful mistake" in 1.8 was "to voamit" (again reading irony into the poem). The final version of 1.8 begins "to lue him?..."

21 Jan 81

These are four well-chosen sonnets. "Cain" is very fine, telling the teacher that the persona of the poem knows Cain better than he does, having been made sometimes more like him by wine. And it makes a good pair with 158, all about wine's marvellously good effects. I like your "slash, slash" and I'm glad it fitted the line. I thought our expression "see red" would do for the water-melons. I've heard about that "est-est," but don't know where, maybe just in an advertisement. Curious how the word for "dry" (of wine) is used in Italian and French, and in other languages, I daresay. I find it's the same in German (trocken). Difficult to find an inviting word for the opposite of *sweet*.

I gave three of these recent ones to Kay Butler for her Stockbridge magazine. She does a lot to make things more interesting for the people of Stockbridge, who like to regard themselves as villagers, I think.

Without wanting to bother you, I shall always be glad to have more.

P.S. In 57 I couldn't manage a word for *boccia*, so made it *pony* (⅓ of a pint, I think, or maybe ¼: they would sell you a pony of beer during the Depression in the Thirties, just an excuse to come in from the cold). So it had to be malt whisky for this *papa* in the sonnet, who doesn't seem hard-up.

I wonder if "the beads" is better than "your beads"? Of more accepted importance, I think.

Note: "Cain" is No. 180.
Kay Butler should read Kay Butcher and the magazine is called *Graffiti*.

5 Feb 81

Thank you for the last three translations: here is 287, a specially good choice. I have been doing these less thick and fast, partly because I had been getting excessive, and also I feared to pester you. So if all goes well, I shall send them after longer intervals, a good number of them at a time. But here is this one by itself, to show that things are still going on.

P.S. Jamieson describes *strone* as somewhat copious, so here its qualifying adjective had better be excused as some figure of speech, I don't know which.

6 Feb 81

I am delighted to tell you that M. Macdonald phoned to tell me he means to publish a book of our Belli translations, with your introduction. He means to add the 52 sonnets in the *Collected Poems* to the new ones we provide, a joint production with both our names on the title-page. I hoped to send you No. 311 as a sign of progress, but have got all taiglit with Nina and Nannarella and Nunziatina. Here is the octave so far as it goes:

This month syne I hae sent the youngest wean[1]
til the wee, faur-back Brithers' Schuil, I'm shair
he'll dae aa richt, screives pat-heuks, wi his quill[2]
and chants the easy nummers by his lane.

Yin's been to Daddie John's a year and mair,
maks umberellies, tither's hewing stane
at St. Michael's, the Orphanage has taen
the auldest laddie, they lairn him Latin thair.[3]

1. pronounced *wane*.
2. too fussy? No, I think not.
3. I like that — not in Belli, though.

Hingers (hangers) were the lines ⌐ and pat-hooks were ⌐
as taught to Scottish infants. I still use my father's pot-hooks when
I have painting to do, on a ladder.

I can see Nannarella should be Annie, to rhyme with grannie, but
I regret it looks as if she will have to have passed awa, and
Nunziatina (or Ina?) is being taen care of by her grannie. But it's
too late for any more tonight.

Note: in l.3 above "wi his quill" was changed to "pretty fair."

20 Feb. 81

Here are the latest three, with much thanks. No. 233 was
difficult, and I hope it does not show too much sign of struggle. I
was determined to get that wonderful line 6 nearly word for
word....

Lines Review (March, I think) is to have two of our Belli sonnets
and one of my Edinburgh sonnets.... And some day *PN Review* is
due to have three Belli sonnets likewise.

I get more and more keen on having a good-sized book of the
new translations with your introduction and one at least in the
original to let people see how the romanesco looks.

P.S. I read a fair selection of the recent translations at a reading in
Dundee University last week, and there was a good deal of interest.

Note: No. 233 is "Think for a Year and a Day Afore ye Tak a Wife," and the second
stanza goes:

> The auld wife fuffs and fluthers like a deil,
> the young ane has got Satan in her erse:
> wi thaim twa randies dancing sic a reel,
> somebody's gauntae leave here in a hearse.

Thank you for these two sonnets, both good ones. 311 makes a pair with 1981, of which Alastair Mackie sent me an English translation he had found, from which I made this version:

THREE LADDIES AND NINE LASSIES

Talk about weans—yon yin had a dizzen
but got them aa set-up aa richt, nae fears!
Sandy and Giulio hae gane fir freres
Gussie's at Terracina; he's in prison,

Clelia dee'd last year, Sarrie has risen
in life, mairriet a bleacher, it appears,
Virginia's been in sairvice twa-three years—
some abbots—wadnae caa the Queen her cousin.

Meenie's a monkrie-houskeeper, nae lack
of gear, Brigit's weit-nurse til an Inglesa,
Amalia has gaed aff wi a quack:

Fermina duis brodderie in gowd; and even
twa mair of them, Cleofe and Teresa,
tho neither has a tredd, can mak a levin.

I think *to learn* (= *to teach*) is considered good usage in Scots (No. 311).

The puns in 304 will take some doing, but we'll see. What a final line!

We should still manage to produce these, even if you are in Suffolk.

Note: No. 311 is "The Weedie wi Sevin Bairns," and the reference is to 1.8.
No. 304 is "The Deidlie Sins," which ends:

Whan Gode plenishit the warld, it appeiris,
wi guid confessors, hummil penitents,
the deil, eenow, creatit nuns and freiris.

Many thanks for a fine lot of good sonnets. These should keep me out of mischief for a while.

No, I daresay we can't exclude the obscene sonnets altogether, I agree. In an American university they would work out the right ratio by computer, but maybe we could have the obscene ones a little below the correct proportion.

One thing beats me with the enclosed translation 304: I had to use *liquorice* instead of *sugaraully*, the word we always used as children, and still current. Strange how the octave gave me a terrible amount of trouble (largely caused by struggles to fit in the word *sugaraully*) but the sestet fell into place of its own accord, the Muse having realised how hard a trauchle this one was.

I am curious about the sin of footsy-footsy. It seems to be "the collision of feet that lovers make as a secret sign." There is a rascally trick, but not one for lovers, of pushing somebody's back foot gently with the next step. Years and years ago, I remember this being done to me in Soho, London, in rather a quiet back-street, so I took no notice.

P.S. *re* No. 360, I wonder about some details. We can check them later. Maybe I depart too far with my stick of rhubarb.

Note: No. 360 is "Wha Gaes by Nicht, Gaes til his Death."

26 March 81

Thank you for this morning's well-chosen and generous selection. Here are copies of translations finished so far, a very interesting batch. 567 is a marvellous sonnet, the original, I mean, though I'm proud of my part of the proceed procdings (can't spell that!) proceedings (I looked it up) as a *tour de force*. Funny how this expression we so often use seems more complimentary in French than it would in English. No. 675 is an especially fine sonnet. Indeed, this is a good mixture of the serious and the cynical, etc. 378 is very amusing. I wonder if there is one about a widow or a widower who has lost the hope of ever being happy again?

Note: No. 567 is "The Rosary at Hame."
No. 675 is "A Stecht Painch Duisnae Trow a Tuim Ane."
No. 378 is "Weedoheid."

170

I can't resist sending this first more-or-less fair copy of 974. I've copied it into the notebook but it isn't typed yet and I'm not doing it to-night, no thanks! Also, these others are ready for typing:

658 ["Jyle"], 377 ["The Condiment of Paradise"], 879 ["The New Quack"], 1004 ["The Sairvant that Tined (her) Job"], 886 ["The Sooth"], and 897 ["The Fletherer"].

Anyone can see I have just had fun with 974 ["The Apostles' Vaige"]; made a kind of holiday of it, and I don't care.

Please may I have some more? There is only one left.

P.S. I hope these towns are pronounced Stórta, Báccano, Mónterósi, otherwise rhyme b4 is done for.

I'll send some translations to the magazine *Stand*. They have just asked me to renew my subscription, so these can accompany it and so we'll wait and see what will happen.

Note: Nos. 575, 740 and 854 were published posthumously in *Stand*.

1 April 81

I was delighted to receive the latest batch of ten, just when I had written to ask for more. Now I had better not bother you for a while. I hope you will find a house that you like. Heading south does look a good idea on a day like this here. I have sent three sonnets to Jon Silkin for his magazine *Stand* (with my subscription that was due), as broad a hint as one could make. But he had asked me to send something.

I very much appreciate all this help. There are now 59 sonnets not in the *Collected Poems*, all but one, I think, done with your help. I don't know how many to aim at for M. Macdonald's projected book. I shall phone and ask him. Total now 111, not bad at all, except by G. G. Belli's standards.

P.S. I got thoroughly in a fang or fankle or taigle or just plain tangle with the rhymes in No. 974, and let it go as a bit of fun.

Nine Book Reviews

ROBERT GARIOCH SUTHERLAND
MAKAR 1909–1981
BADE HERE

THESE WI THREE CHUCKIE-STANES
I LAY ON SCOTLAND'S CAIRN

THE SALTIRE SOCIETY 1983

from a photograph by Robin Fulton

Leanings

THE PENGUIN BOOK OF SCOTTISH VERSE
Edited and introduced by Tom Scott.

This anthology has an attractive cover, a reproduction of Raeburn's painting of the Rev. Robert Walker skating on Duddingston Loch. It has been chosen with some subtlety. Painted probably in 1784, it shows the minister, very sure of himself, well-balanced on one leg and leaning slightly to the left. He does not seem to be on record as a poetry-lover, but he did write a book about "kolf" on his return from a visit to Holland. He was a member of the Skating Society, the Wagering Club and the Royal Company of Archers, and would be one of those whom Dr Scott, equally self-confident and leaning very evidently to the left, describes as "the philistine Edimbourgeoisie" who "treated Burns little better than they did Fergusson."

Dr Scott has done his work *con amore*, which implies hatred of those he suspects of failing to share his love. In reply to anyone who would prefer the more balanced attitude of a neat literary historian, we may suggest that Dr Scott's posture promises at least a certain liveliness. Let us say at once that this book is what it presumably sets out to be: a useful introductory anthology, though we reserve doubts so far as recent poetry is concerned. It is not meant for scholars: texts are not named and the spelling is simplified on a plan quite suitable for the purpose of this book, and defended with perhaps unnecessary heat: "I have taken the step of trying to apply this principle of a standard Scots to the great pre-Reformation writers, where possible. This will be anathema to purist academics who set textual idolatry above true worship of the living poem, but this book is not intended for purist academics." Fair enough, we may say, it's not a book for scholars. This quotation, incidentally, shows other characteristics besides the peppery kind: the use of the word "Reformation" to mark the end of the Middle Ages, and the religious intensity of Dr Scott's approach to his subject. These and other idiosyncrasies will irritate readers who like an anthology to be simply businesslike and factual. This one, indeed, is businesslike on the whole, the moralistic critic takes over only sometimes from the scholar that Dr Scott obviously is. Some may even enjoy the quarrelsome bits, but others will heed this warning. Dr Scott gives

175

a good account of the history of the Scots language. Barbour is described as using "the Northumberland dialect spoken from the Humber to Aberdeen," And "the national language," he tells us, becomes identifiable "in Henrysoun's time or earlier."

To prepare an anthology of a whole literature cannot be easy: some poets and certain of their works leave no alternatives, but a very wide choice remains. Leaving the last half-century for later consideration, we find most of the things that we would expect. The book is specially commended for including also specimens of William Wilkie, Maidment's *Pasquils, The Merry Muses, Anster Fair* and modern folk-songs. It does well to place in that unhappy gap about the middle of the 19th century an extract from Alexander Smith's "Glasgow." The popular Charles Murray is taken seriously, as he ought to be. I think it is wrong to leave out the *Moralitas* from each of Henryson's *Fables* (I can't get used to Dr Scott's spelling) on grounds that "for readers of poetry for its own sake, the lily of the tale needs no gilding."

This is surely a very odd remark. And an even odder thing about this whole book is its very close similarity to *The Oxford Book of Scottish Verse*, chosen by John MacQueen and Tom Scott, published four years ago. Very often we find that all, or nearly all, the examples of a certain poet are already in the *Oxford Book*, which generally has more besides. This is not so much the case with Henryson and Gavin Douglas, and the *Penguin Book* has four by William Dunbar not in the *Oxford Book*, but of the Bannatyne and Maitland MSS anonymous poems, Oxford has all the Penguin examples and a good many in addition. The same is true of Alexander Montgomerie, and of the Ballads, except for "The Douglas Tragedy." Of the 20 Burns poems in Penguin, 17 are in Oxford. For Fergusson the proportion is 5:3; for Hogg, 4:3; for the voluminous Walter Scott, 6:6. The same extracts are given of "King Berdok," and of "Colkelbie Sow," except that of the latter Oxford gives a bigger helping.

No poet is included who was born later than 1928; this may be practical, but the last few get very scanty treatment accompanied by unhelpful notes, which perhaps we need not particularise, except to say that an uninitiated reader will get no inkling of the variety and quality of the work of Alexander Scott, Edwin Morgan, George Mackay Brown, Burns Singer and Iain Crichton Smith, the last five in the anthology. We notice that Crichton Smith's "Culloden and

After" has nine more lines in the Oxford book than in the Penguin. Of course, he may have deleted them on second thoughts but we don't know.

It may be asking too much, but it would have been better to give a fair showing to poems written in the last five years or so. A lot of things are going on right here and now that are exciting, or one would think, from Dr Scott's point of view, at least disturbing. As it is, the uninitated reader, who will presumably buy this book, may get the completely wrong impression that poetry in Scotland has nearly petered out.

—The Listener, 14 May 1970

CLYTACH
By Alastair Mackie (Akros Publications).

There is an encouraging feeling of confidence about this collection, notwithstanding a recurrent type of poem, expressive of misgivings, that we shall have to consider later. It is evident that Alastair Mackie knows what he is about, is aware of problems and has a fair idea of how to tackle them. He is responsible, serious and competent. His purpose is to make poems, not to bring us any message, to hector us or heckle, to look impressive or to obtrude his personality. He is aware that poems are made of words with single or multiple meanings and with their sounds, their family histories and infinite possibilities or relationships. Words have their associations also, and mysterious powers; a special problem arises here, as the collection is all in Scots, and the impression of confidence comes largely from Mr Mackie's approach to this. It is a real problem, as a disproportionately large number of words must come directly from books, though it has been over-emphasised for many years by those who doubt the usefulness of literary Scots.

Mr Mackie has not been prolific so far, but this is a good sign under these circumstances. There are twenty-eight poems in this volume, which is not very many, and only six of them run on to a second page, but every one is worth taking seriously. Their subject-matter is resourceful, varied and interesting; even "Orpheus and

Euridice" and "Frae Penelope" are not quite what one would expect, and "The Models," for example, is quite out of the ordinary—

> Wheesht! the models are listening till their claes
> i the skyrie salons o the magazines.

That is perhaps something like the kind of way in which Apollinaire's (or Donne's?) mind worked; it is certainly a remarkable thought to come into anyone's head.

The metre is perhaps the least interesting element here, but at least the poems are not uniformly in ordinary free verse; they vary greatly in appearance and have some rhythmic interest. "Still-Life: Cezanne," in fact, gains greatly from having a regular form from which to deviate in a comprehensible manner. It is a sonnet, and a good one too in its way. The words also may be generally relied upon to make an interesting sound.

Let us first consider more closely two poems that particularly express misgivings, because the whole collection depends on how these doubts should be dealt with. Of these, "Through the Deid-Chack" comes first in this volume, and "Scots Pegasus" not last, significantly, but second-last. The deid-chack is the sound he is making, but he tells us so only in the last (two-word) line of this sixteen-line poem. It is a strange poem, and frightening, in a way, with its terrible words: *deid-chack* (sound made by wood worm, a death omen) and *deid-ruckle* (death-rattle). These meanings are all quoted from the *Word Leet* (Glossary). I wish *wood worm* had been *death watch beetle*, more accurate and associated with even greater destruction, but that is by the way. The poem's logic works all right, but in a series of jerks. He huddles in the midst of a dying language that says little except *clytach* (barbarous speech)—an "auld body / aince a horizon / noo a pirlicue." This last is the poem's key-word, one of many in the book that are new to me and well worth learning. Its meaning is "space between thumb and middle finger when fully extended" so it is one of those Scots words that have no English equivalent. (It is not in S.N.D. or Jamieson.) The poem gives out a gleam of hope, since a pirlicue has room "for nieve poems / gowpens o auld-farrant wirds" but this is immediately followed by the comfortless ending—"Tho I hear the deid-chack / I mak." "Scots Pegasus" is simpler, almost comically apologetic for that non-starter with "yon etten and spewed look" (a marvellous

178

expression!) Only some magic or miracle could get him off the ground, but there is no chance of that—"naebody, dammt, kens the horseman's wird" (secret word passed on by horsemen to ensure mastery of the horse). But after this comes "Probe," a fine concluding poem. The poet is deafened by languages coming in on the wireless from all over the world, but—

> at the hinner end
> my wave linth dirls wi Lallans.
>
> I mak oot the shaky trimmles.
> I get the clash o the toun.

The rest of this collection shows that he can make good use of this clash (talk). He is steadily making good poems with a very rich vocabulary. A glossary of over 500 words is provided on a separate sheet, which would be convenient except that it is in necessarily small type, on unnecessarily green paper, that hardly shows up at a yard's distance from a 100-watt light. Apart from that, it is no trouble at all to look up his words. I cannot see why anyone should blench at this light task, or object to an author's use of a dictionary in any language, unless he uses words crudely and without skill, but that would make him a bad writer in any case. There can be no possible objection of this kind to Alastair Mackie's use of unfamiliar words. Let him keep at it, and they will become familiar. Even his glossary is interesting in itself, and almost complete; of that I am reasonably certain. His words stand up pretty well to a close look, so well, in fact, that it seems worthwhile to call attention to a few that have puzzled me. *Brodheids* (nails) are not in Jamieson, S.N.D. nor D.O.S.T. *Brod* is a spike, or it may be a board, so Jamieson gives *brodheid* as a board-head. All the same, Mr Mackie makes a splendid concluding line of it—"afore the brodheids hemmert doun the nicht." *Pirlicue*—see above— does not seem to have the required meaning, though *pirlie* is the familiar *pinkie*, or little finger, and here we may have some local usage worth hearing about. I was doubtful about the three following words, but found them all vindicated. *Laggans o the air* (horizon) turns up as a Number 3 usage in the S.N.D., which also has *gey* as an adjective. *Heuch* (sickle) appears as a variant spelling in S.N.D., and is not a double misprint as I had feared. *Nieve* (punch) still puzzles me, however, as it seems to mean nothing but the familiar fist. *Nevel* (blow with the fist) is in Jamieson, S.N.D. and D.O.S.T. (in preparation). Would that be a better word?

In "Châteaux en Ecosse," a particularly good poem that is a key to the whole book, Mr Mackie tells how his grandmother used such expressions as *puffin-lowe* (flame) and *widden-dremers* (those who see visions in firelight), new to me at least, but easily understood as compounds. What is specially good about this poem is that it shows how certain words can gather other words about them, so that the poem forms itself under the author's control. He is in his grandmother's house—"the deid auld body, my grandmither / croonin tae the firelicht unkent wirds." Each stanza has a line of conversation, so they are all linked, and also has comments that build up the fireside scene, the atmosphere of which is nicely conveyed (Mr Mackie is pictorially very skilful) with the associations of the words set in history, all in a few lines—"It was her deid forebears . . . brekkin oot o history and their crubbit lives . . ." and this neatly-constructed poem, having started with the *puffin-lowe*, ends thus—

> Here's me blawin on the cauld ess o her tongue
> tae bigg, châteaux en Ecosse, thae bit poems.

It may be helpful to point out a few more objects of interest that the reader will be pleased to find. That poem with the *brodheids* in the last line is "Weet Kin," one of the recurrent poems in which Scotland and Scots, for the time being, seem pretty nearly hopeless—"Ach, Scotland, a back close i the mind, / the doup o the seck, let doun country." But it gives a vivid impression of the birds singing in a wet May before the last line puts a stop to them. "New Moon" also makes a powerful effect out of an ordinary natural occurrence by means of unusual but unforced imagery—"Heuch edge o ice; / the fremmit rim o a Mongol shield . . ." Imaginative imagery of a quite different kind but equally original, is exactly suited to a football poem, "Drappit"—"The goalie's like a bloke that's crucifeet . . ." and to "Pietà" in which a child killed in an air-raid has "hippens for deid claes." "Still-Life: Cezanne" is startlingly unusual: the painter is hard put to it to keep his unruly collection of objects where he wants them on the canvas, but manages in the end by glowering at them. There is plenty more variety here, however. Let us hope that Mr Mackie will get the misgivings out of his system and go ahead to do the difficult task for which he is much needed. He will, too. He has not got the horseman's magic word, but that is because there is really no such thing, as any skilful and hard-working and indispensable plewman could have told you.

—*Lines Review*, 42-43, 1973

PAUCAE MICAE (A FEW CRUMBS)
By William Christie (Castlelaw Press).

This 20-page pamphlet, beautifully produced as we have come to expect of Alex Frizzell's press, offers eight paraphrases from Horace and one four-line poem of Sappho, all in the dialect of the Mearns. Unassumingly titled, these are crumbs from a high-quality loaf, or bannock, rather, since the language, names, rhythms, atmosphere, and perhaps the Horatian practical wisdom, are all associated with the Mearns, whatever they may or may not have to do with the Sabine farm. The poems are not presented as translations, and even as paraphrases they are subjected in places to a process that comes of Mr Christie's own mental activity. For instance in *Odes* II, 10, Horace has: "Whoso cherishes the golden mean, safely avoids the foulness of an ill-kept house and discreetly too, avoids a hall exciting envy" (Bennett), whereas Mr Christie enlarges upon these terse statements:

Fa ever tries to haud the mids, he'll hae nae orra biggin'
Wi' broken door an' rantle tree, an' reekit thack for riggin';
He winna ware hard-won bawbees to busk ower braw his hoose—

It just gars folk envy ye, man, gin e'er ye craw ower crouse.

This does not happen every time, however; the eight lines of *Odes* I, 38, become eight lines of neatly-turned Scots, the Mediterranean details nicely acclimatised, so that the *thick-leaved vine* is left out of the scenery and *bibentem*, on the other hand, is particularised by the specification of *barley bree*. Another neat, economical and delightful "paraphrase" is made of *Odes* IV, 7. It is in fact a nearly exact translation, so far as such a thing is a possibility in verse: *decrescentia flumina* becomes *spateless burns*, and *mutat terra . . .* is beautifully turned as "The earth her goon has changed again."
    The style throughout is assured, as it has to be where Horace is

concerned. Gracefulness and polish and suavity are characteristics somewhat foreign to the Mearns folk and to their language; what is rather to be expected is a certain dignity and comeliness, decency of arrangement and honest detail, such as you find in those coloured drawings of farmhorses in their harness. Such excellent qualities are to be found in Mr Christie's work, which confidently takes its place in the tradition of presenting Horace in a Scottish setting. Allan Ramsay was perhaps the first, and has not been excelled. Fergusson also did it well. R. L. Stevenson and Charles Murray made useful contributions, J. Logie Robertson did not translate Horace; his method was to select a phrase as a starting-point for a poem of his own, presented in the character of "Hugh Haliburton," an Ochils shepherd, and he made such a good job of it that "Hughie" became popular, especially with country people, including real Ochils shepherds.

The late John A. Birkbeck, in his introduction to *Paucae Micae*, reminds us that "It is fitting that Horace, who was a farmer, should be translated into a country dialect," and thus he adds his bit to the tradition which may always have included this idea, though Horace was a "gentleman farmer" and welcome in the imperial palace where homespun would not be worn. In fact, J. Logie Robertson's poems did not present Horace in homespun, but "Hughie" as a shepherd whose moderate habits of thought had something in common with those of Horace.

Mr Christie has continued successfully with such an attitude, but with a practice of translation more on the lines of those other poets of this tradition. He wisely uses verse-forms familiar to readers of Scots poetry, though perhaps not always appositely, as in the case of our first quotation, the quatrains of whose fourteeners are very different from the original stanzas, though mostly his metres correspond rather well.

The language is very satisfying, handled without awkwardness, showing not only skill in versification but easy familiarity with the words. *Scorth* puzzled me till I noticed *scorg*—a jagged rock, in the glossary provided by John A. Birkbeck, who explains: "I have not hesitated to consult the author rather than to rely on a reference to Jamieson." Such reference, however, reveals that Jamieson is very much in agreement with Mr Christie and indicates that a large number of Mr Christie's words are familiar in the North-east.

—*Lines Review* 44, 1973

SELECTION OF POEMS BY WILLIAM BARNES
Edited by Robert Nye (Fyfield Books, Carcanet Press).

If the subject is poetry, and William Barnes is mentioned, do you automatically add: "the Dorset poet"? There is no harm if this is just a label, but the important point is that he was a poet, and a good one too, who preferred to use his "mother tongue," as he called it in the preface to the 1862 collection, here quoted by Robert Nye in his excellent Introduction. Barnes is referring to his Dorset dialect, which he says some might deem "a fast out-wearing speech-form." He says further in *An Outline of English Speech-craft*, quoted on the fly-leaf of this helpfully-planned volume: "I have shapen my teaching as that of a speech of breath-sounded words, and not of lettered ones." As Robert Nye points out, "it is impertinent to praise or blame him as a 'Dorset poet', a poet whose relevance is local."

Some of the poems here are in English, managed, at its best, as beautifully perhaps as Gray's "Elegy," possibly with an added technical element learned from his interest in Welsh poetry, which is mentioned in the Introduction:

> The horses now have left their rolling wheels
> And reel'd in home to stable, to their stalls,

and to his native Dorset dialect he brings the same craftsmanship, with a new kind of music that was much needed in the first half of the nineteenth century:

> An' he had sich a bit o' fun!
> He meäde the maïdens squeäl an' run,
> Because 'twer Easter Zunday.

There is much fun in the dialect poems, but this voice can give perfect expression also to simple human grief, as in the first stanza of "The Wife a-Lost":

> Since I noo mwore do zee your feäce,
> Up steäirs or down below,
> I'll zit me in the lwonesome pleäce,
> Where flat-bough'd beech do grow;
> Below the beeches' bough, my love,
> Where you did never come,
> An' I don't look to meet ye now,
> As I do look at hwome.

A lot of skill, as well as feeling, has gone into the writing of this apparently simple poem. The last two lines are repeated with variations, in all four stanzas. This has the effect of tightening the whole poem so that it encloses a kind of perfect hopelessness. The short repeated concluding line is another of the not extraordinary devices that he uses to remarkable effect. The "Easter Zunday" poem, for instance, starts thus:

> Last Easter Jim put on his blue
> Frock cwoat, the vu'st time—vier new;
> Wi' yollow buttons all o' brass,
> that glitter'd in the zun lik' glass;

This goes on to make up a stanza or section of fourteen lines, with a list of his items of holiday finery, except that the last line is what we have been waiting for without knowing it: the (virtually) six-syllable part of a fourteener. Then he does exactly the same with the second section, with a list of the things Jim did and saw. So the whole thing is a kind of suspension of a ballad stanza, made of two sections of fourteen lines each; a more artful affair than one might have expected from this talk of *laggens* and *kitty-boots*.

He can work wonders, also, with scraps of talk that he has very likely overheard. In "The Heare—Dree o'm a-takèn o't," his three numbered characters give an exciting radio-style commentary on a hare's escape from the greyhounds, in heroic couplets!

> (2) There, I do zee em over-right thik cow.
> (3) The red woone?
>   (1) No, a mile beyand her now.

and in a poem with the delightful title, "A Lot o' Maïdens a-Runnèn the Vields" we have a talking-picture of some girls out for a walk till a thunderstorm sends them scampering. It is all done by means of direct speech, mostly one speech to a line, with much Hee! Hee! and Oh! Oh!, all great fun and true to every detail.

The general effect is one of sturdy self-reliant people who enjoy life and do not ask for much, like the small farmer, proud of his "Hwome-stead":

> I'm landlord o' my little farm,
>   I'm king 'ithin my little pleäce:
> I don't break laws, an' don't do harm,
>   An' ben't afeärd o' noo man's feäce.

They can quarrel, though, especially if their ability as workers is challenged; then they call one another, "You yoppen dog!" or "You snub-nos'd flopperchops!" though in the main they are friendly folk.

But much depends on the "squier," and there are bad squires as well as good. And Barnes is aware of the threats of enclosures of the common land. He deals with this dark side of rural life mainly in his eclogues, in some of which the conversation of his real country folk becomes distressingly topical. "Eclogue: The Common a-Took In" starts with a man's simple question to his friend: why is he carrying such a load of geese? What follows is heartrending, with no trace of self-pity or even of vindictiveness. He must sell his geese because the common moor is to be enclosed, and his "little cow" will have to go, and all. He has been managing quite well; with the cow put on the common in summer, his bit of grass could grow and he could make a rick of hay. The geese yielded him quills and feathers and food—"to zell to gentlevo'ks." Some good squires have been letting allotments to the poor—another eclogue describes a happy man who has one—but failing this, the only prospect is the workhouse.

William Barnes' dialect-writing was based on scholarship as well as personal knowledge. The list of his published works in the Editor's Note—one of the many useful features in this well-arranged book—takes up nearly a page. They include *A Grammar and Glossary of the Dorset Dialect* (1864). Mr Nye tells us how particular Barnes was with the spelling of the word *geäte*, when dictating his last poem to his daughter. " 'That is how King Alfred would have pronounced it,' he said." We are scarcely aware of his scholarship, however, when reading the poems, delighting in his technical skill and humane interests and fun, and notably in his prevailing health and good-humour. For though his range embraces tragedy and exposes cruelty, greed and patient suffering at the hands of unthinking squires, his usual attitude is:

"There's nothen vor to mwope about."

—*Lines Review* 45, 1973

GLASGOW SONNETS
By Edwin Morgan (Castlelaw Press).

This is a sixteen-page pamphlet from the Castlelaw Press, which
lately has produced smallish books with such frequency that it may
be taken seriously as a new Scottish publishing-house. The present
sample of its work is printed with loving care by Alex M. Frizzell
on good paper with really black ink supplemented on the title-page
with red to match the cover, very neat, with clean, classic type of
generous size, nicely spaced, one sonnet to a page.

  These ten Italian-type sonnets, each set out in workmanlike
fashion as a solid block of fourteen lines, were written in nine days,
an enviable production-rate rivalling that of Giuseppe Belli.
Together they make a well-ordered sequence out of the public
material of Glasgow as it is right now, beginning with the dirty old
streets that are being cleared away, going on to consider the clean
lines of structures that are replacing them, together with attempts
here and there to clean old buildings and prop them up, and ending
with misgivings about the brave new Glasgow that is beginning to
appear. The book is full of a purposeful energy characteristic of
Glasgow, but accompanied with a keen intelligence lacking,
perhaps, in a city that is confidently building very high multi-storey
flats on the same unproved principles that are being applied
everywhere else. So these sonnets are right up to date, and located
exactly in space. Meanwhile, people are living in this uncouth
environment, and it is with people that Edwin Morgan is mostly
concerned. If there is anything in the idea that certain subjects are
particularly suitable for verse, surely this is one of them.

  One thing that gives the Sonnet its peculiar properties for us is,
I think, the rhyme-scheme, more difficult and important in Scots or
English than in its native Italian. We may write smooth sonnets by
using dull and plentiful rhymes, but Mr Morgan prefers to tease our
interest by using words of rarer sound, placing an extraordinary
word first as though it were there inevitably, and then introducing
words that seem to fit in easily, or else delighting us with seemingly
superhuman efforts. So Sonnet VIII starts in a fine confident
manner that leads to difficult rhyming territory—"Meanwhile the
flyovers breed loops of light / in curves that would have ravished
tragic Toshy. . . ." Only Toshy will serve here; what is to be done?
Well, we have *wishy-washy* (nae bother—two more to go), then the

virtuosic *Sauchie Hauch she* in the best position for that sort of thing, with *sploshy* coming in without fuss to conclude this part of the performance. All this showing-off is artistically justified, as the poem is about these daring new structures that appear to have insufficient visible means of support. It is a clever and note-worthy poem, with allusions that perhaps need explanations for the benefit of non-Glaswegians and/or non-erudite readers: who is Madame Emé; what are ukiyo-e?

These confident and curiously gay sonnets VIII and IX are well-placed. Sonnet IX is a delight, a marvel and a lesson. Sonnet X also is clever: "A multi is a sonnet stretched to ode / and some say that's no joke. . . ." But wit gives way before thoughts of living in those multi-storey flats, and the sequence ends with the plain and sombre lines: ". . . and when they trudge / from closemouth to launderette their steady shoes / carry a world that weighs us like a judge."

Sonnet VII turns, for a change, from the dismal streets that nobody could love except perhaps for some of their associations, to the Victorian office-buildings which in Glasgow are exceptionally splendid and plentiful. They are all fakes to Mr Morgan, and perhaps a Venetian palace outside of Venice is a fake, however real it may seem to us. He would not like to see the façade of the Stock Exchange when it was held up on steel crutches while they built a new office-block on to the back of it. This sort of thing has evoked some fine lines: "Prop up's the motto. Splint the dying age. / Never displease the watchers from the grave."

Sonnet VI starts with a striking, imaginative and actual image: "The North Sea oil-strike tilts East Scotland up, / and the great sick Clyde shivers in its bed." It goes on to gloomy thoughts of miserable lives. I wonder if here the rhymes slip over the edge of awkwardness, *e.g. on fled- / from trees*. The hyphen does not help, certainly, being separated from *fled* by a distinct space, a peculiarity of this otherwise practical and beautiful hand-printing.

Sonnet III is technically remarkable, having Glaswegian direct speech in addition to English narrative. Its rhymes are managed easily and inconspicuously, so the iambic pentameters become of additional interest, varying just sufficiently to carry the speech-rhythm: " 'Ye can take it or leave it but. The position / is simple, you want a hoose. I say / for eight hundred pounds it's yours. . . .' "

Sonnets I and VI add up to give a powerful impression of Glasgow in grim past days and in queer, inhuman, transitional modern times. Brilliance is held in restraint to be displayed in the climactic, or pseudo-climactic, Sonnets VIII and IX. So there is order throughout the sequence, though one suspects that if the gay and confident climax is really an interpolation, the order is perhaps uneasy, as is our trust in town-planning however hopefully we may think from time to time.

—*Lines Review* 45, 1973

Michael Hamburger—Memoirs and Poems

A MUG'S GAME: INTERMITTENT MEMOIRS 1924-1954
OWNERLESS EARTH: NEW AND SELECTED POEMS
(Carcanet Press).

It is of unusual interest to find a volume of *New and Selected Poems* appearing at almost the same time as the poet's *Memoirs*; especially as Michael Hamburger's life, it is clear, is altogether related to poetry. (Even his Army diaries, he tells us, were filled with literary notes "and almost total lack of response to what was going on around him.") Here, we may think, is an opportunity to find answers to the questions: how is a poem conceived?—can it be written to order? Of course, we find no simple answers in *A Mug's Game* though many allusions may be traced. Mr Hamburger does give details of his life-story that are connected with certain poems, but he has excluded most of these poems from *Ownerless Earth* and gives reasons why he has found them wanting. He is very well aware of these questions, however, and tries to help us with what answers he can find out of his experience.

> The great mystery of the written word . . . lies in its power to oppose biological time, to create its own time dimension, the dimension that distinguishes human beings from animals. . . . If anybody ever feels like taking the trouble to look at my poems in the light of the little I remember of my life . . . he or she will find superficial traces in them of my army experience; but the real sources, connections and developments are underground. My guess about them would be no better than his or hers.

Early in his poetic life, Mr Hamburger had come to believe what friends had told him: that he was not good at writing elegiac poetry, or any other kind required for a special occasion. He tells us how reluctant he was to accept a commission "to write a tribute to T. S. Eliot for his sixtieth birthday." Inhibited by the idea of writing a poem to order, even in praise of a man he greatly admired, he hesitated till it was almost too late for the deadline (Tambimuttu wished to publish it, with other such poems, in a book) and was about to refuse finally, when "the poem was suddenly there." It was a very good poem, too, true but not obvious in its thought-processes, as we can see for ourselves, since it is in *Ownerless Earth*.

There is often somewhere in people's minds a preconception of something peculiar, fascinating and even alarming about the life of a poet, and not only that of a "romantic"; we may not take Murger or Berlioz too seriously in this respect, but what about Dr Johnson's *Lives*? Well, here is Michael Hamburger, in 1941, aged 17 (he is helpful with dates, though his "intermittent memoirs" do hop about in time), when he had recently left Westminster School "as soon as possible, so as to get a taste of independence at Oxford before joining up," already a poet and a translator of Hölderlin, "with an image of velvet jackets as emblems of the artistic life," left by a performance of *La Bohème*, his first opera, to which his grandfather had taken him before 1936, very pleased when his sister Maria introduced him to David Gascoyne and another friend (whom he calls "X"), ". . . the first poet I had met, and all that my adolescent notions told me a poet ought to be . . . he knew the strangest people I had ever heard about before my own excursions into London bohemia."

From then till 1954, he lets us follow his life, at Oxford and in the Army for four years, and back in Oxford; then through years of taking things as they came, with innumerable meetings and conversations, much travel, never free from anxiety nor from its own kind of restrictions; and yet when for a time he had a steady job as university lecturer, there were reasons, which he makes plain to us, why that secure and gainful occupation was less desirable than his style of *la vie de bohème*.

His explanation is very interesting to us, if one of our principal concerns as his readers is the insight he gives us into the way people use their lives, which never seem to be long enough (though several of the people he mentions did shorten theirs deliberately) and what anyone, especially a poet, has to show for some particular stretch of his time. Extensive passages from Mr Hamburger's diary for 1950 supply much material of this kind:

> Nov. 18: On Tuesday, after a lesson in the morning, went to Oxford to give a talk on Edwin Muir's poetry . . . went to John Donne's rooms to drink, then to a pub with him, Watt and Martin Seymour-Smith. Dined at the Taj . . . Slept in Oriel guest room, began to write poem. Can't get away from obession with time, change. . . . After breakfast went to Elinor's barge, talked, went out to her Department. Quarrelled over her fellow anthropologists. Went to see Franz Baermann Steiner . . . Strange effect Oxford has on me since I went down. Tried to render this in poem, but it hasn't come off—so far.

Kathleen Raine, in a letter "as perceptive as it was kind," told him (what may be in most of our minds) that he was "extremely fortunate . . . to command a university teaching job at all . . . one of the least useless things one can do." The obstacles were real enough to him, however; his explanation should be read in full, being too subtle to summarise, or to quote adequately. In short, he says:

> I resisted the pursuit of knowledge as an end in itself—and knowledge of literature at that; when it was the practice of literature that taught how little I knew even about my most intimate and intense concerns. Nor could I have told about the complex of assumptions and obsessions behind that resistance, if only because I couldn't see it myself, until the poems I wrote brought it to light.

Later, he states firmly:

> A poet whose work would not leave me cold must have a core of commitment not necessarily to the "ceremony of innocence" but to innocence itself. (*One Foot in Eden* is the title of Edwin Muir's last book of poems; the other foot can be anywhere, but preferably in a place unmistakably human and not too tidy.)

This is most illuminating, this invocation of Edwin Muir, who lived quietly, spending much of his time in practical jobs, whilst keeping that "core of commitment" that is at the centre also of Murger's bohemians and of Berlioz' fantastic poet.

Certainly, to be a poet on these terms is to live in a state of anxiety about where the next poem is to come from. Perhaps a poet should be defined as a person who has written poems, rather than as one who does; but it is unlikely that he would be pleased at any time to apply this definition to himself. Readers who know about such things will find these memoirs exceedingly interesting in this respect:

> Something had gone wrong with the way my energy was distributed and directed. It wasn't a matter of time. It was a matter of not being able to afford, or feeling that I wasn't able to afford, the blank and passive process of gestation. There was always something on my mind, something that had to be done or thought about. . . . In February, I was still working on the tiny "Spring Song in Winter" that had announced itself between Notting Hill Gate and Tottenham Court Road on December 3rd.

This was during the time of his lectureship at University College, London. But here is an extract from a diary written in Sicily in 1950: "May 18th: . . . Started poem at last . . . May 21st: Done nothing, seen nothing, thought nothing. . . . Poem doesn't progress." Elsewhere he is ready to agree that the world is over-populated with poems; there is no need to worry about keeping up the poetical contribution to the G.N.P. On the other hand, "Joris" was wrong when he told Hamburger, aged 15, in 1939: "You are talking rubbish when you say your life depends on it." ("Joris" was a schoolfellow of his at Westminster, if that word may be applied to a marvellously mature boy, who does not seem to have developed into an unusually mature man. His character-study, developed in the course of many pages dealing with Michael Hamburger's earlier years in London, is one of many subjects that go to make these memoirs so interesting in general.)

But for all these expressions of a poet's diffidence and anxiety, so interesting by virtue of their frankness and urgency, here is *Ownerless Earth*, selected from Mr Hamburger's six previous books of poetry, with twenty-eight poems previously unpublished: as fine an exhibition of confident poetry as we could hope to see, gathered from the output of thirty-one years.

Clarity is the immediately noticeable quality of these poems. You will not need to look up a dictionary; and if that is one of your pleasures, you will forego it meantime. Words are chosen for their meanings, it appears, and yet the verse moves forward confidently, carried upon its rhythm. This example, from "Life and Art I"

191

(*Weather and Season*, 1953), has the strength, I think, of blank verse; it hasn't a single iambic pentameter, but the pattern is there, so that this convincingly casual snatch of conversation has the authority of poetry. That is why we read or listen attentively, as we cannot do with a good deal of verse that we are asked to read, which really is casual and conversational (and negligible). This, I think, distinguishes poetry from prose:

> 'A cell' I reply when visitors remark
> On the small high windows of the room I work in,
> A room without a view. 'Exactly what I need,
> Daylight enough—no more—to push a pen by' . . .

Outside, in the garden, is nature, full of the violence of small creatures. Now Art comes on the scene: his friend Denis Lowson sketches the garden:

> At once I longed to possess it (the garden, the sketch?)
> And above my desk I pinned up the silence extracted
> From the endless commotion of squirrels, jackdaws and owls . . .

So the metaphor is there not because it is striking (which it is: no conceit-specialist ever did better) but because it makes an aesthetic point, and the whole robust poem is there to give that metaphor a solid state in which it can exist. As for the blank verse that never becomes apparent, what the reader is aware of always is the steady rhythm of a very considerable energy working usefully under control.

A Mug's Game quietly tells us some terrible details of his early life in Berlin, shortly before that bad year, 1933, when he found himself, alone with his brother, lost in the corridors of George Watson's College, Edinburgh, knowing no English, sent to find their own way about, their father, who had been a professor of Medicine, too busy to take them to school on their first day, swotting in an unknown language to qualify for a medical practice in Britain, and their mother likewise, struggling to run a house in a foreign country, with little money and the same language difficulty. Shortly before, in the classroom of an early Nazi teacher, he had become aware that he was Jewish, something he had not thought about before: "Suddenly we were Jews—for that teacher's purpose and others not clear to us." And there had been a small, poignant loss on the journey; their German-speaking budgerigar had not been allowed past the Customs. Later, over the years, there were the fragments of news of the immense horrors that were going on in Germany. From his father's mother, though ". . . all those years / She had refused to travel even to save her life" they received a postcard: "Am going on a journey," and that was the last they heard. Out of those things, long after, came poems such as "Treblinka—A Survivor Speaks:" (1959-1969) now newly published:

> That winter night they were burning corpses
> And from the bonfire, flooding the whole camp
> Flared purple and blue and red and orange and gold,
> The many colours of Joseph's coat, who was chosen.

Such a figure of speech is too powerful even to discuss. In this and in a few other poems, he has firmly placed those horrors, fulfilling a task that many good poets could not have brought themselves to carry out; and others, by speaking more loudly, might have done less well. "In a Cold Season," also previously unpublished and in the same group, is a noble poem, explicitly written in our time when words like *noble* have lost their value and have not been replaced. It is a celebration, in fact, of Adolf Eichmann:

> Yet, Muse of the IN-trays, OUT-trays,
> Shall he be left uncelebrated
> For lack of resonant numbers calculated
> To denote your hero, and our abstract age?

So the poem opens thus:

> Words cannot reach him in his prison of words
> Whose words killed men because those men were words
> Women and children who to him were numbers . . .

and the poem leads on to its climax in the death of an old lady whom he killed, a real person to us, made real in a few lines of the poem, though it is a presumed death, a space without news:

> I heard no cry, nor saw her dying face,
> Have never known the place, the day,
> Whether by bullet, gas or deprivation
> They finished her off who was old and ill enough
> To die before long in her own good time;

That was his father's mother, "whom I adored, because she was childlike and did not care about rules and prohibitions." The poem brings her alive in a few lines, but we may learn more about her, in her own surroundings, by reading the memoirs.

"Orpheus Street, S.E.5" (*Travelling*, 1969) evidently began with Mr Hamburger's grasping the possibilities of something observed. This poem about the short and simple street off Denmark Hill starts with thoughts of Orpheus with his lute, playing to "Those houses put up by the money-makers / For the meek, their no-men to breed in. . ." A fantasy follows, all about what Orpheus can do to pavements and trains, till "the whole town swings." But he gets mixed up with traffic diversions which are also his devious way out of the Underworld. And the poem becomes tragic, that had started bizarre; the tragedy of Orpheus is played in Camberwell, which is no more drab, perhaps, than Pluto's domain.

The collection ends with what looks like the beginning of something very big: Sections I to V of a poem called "Travelling." This started as a seemingly self-contained poem, which is now Section I, and surprised him by greatly extending itself into four more sections, without apparently coming near an end. It may be a great crystallisation of those years of travelling of which he gives us so many details in *A Mug's Game*:

> My travels, true, are unlearning,
> An unloading of this piece and that,
> Shedding of names, needs.
> But the last have the pull of earth,
> Of the earth we walk, our foothold.
> Break them, and we fly or go under.

Those travels were not pleasure-trips; he enjoyed what he could as it came, but it was mixed in with much discomfort in third-class carriages abroad, with foreign food and drink and exotic illnesses. He hated Paris and other big towns, and yet he went there. He didn't go in much for sight-seeing, but got mixed up with tourists in Avignon and such places, like Orpheus in the South London traffic. But he collected much experience. Some of it he dutifully recorded in his diary, and worked up into competent prose; and he gives an example of how he did this in *A Mug's Game*, which yields a piece of literature that ought, one thinks, to be part of a very popular story in a paperback with an alluring cover. Now, in "Travelling" those experiences are asserting themselves; or his poetic genuis (I choose this word with care) has taken charge of that rich material.

194

Mr Hamburger has met many people, and in his memoirs he makes them interesting to us in countless passing references. He writes appreciatively of critics whose judgement he has respected and used to his advantage; remembering, for instance, those evenings in Beaufort Street, Chelsea, when G. S. Fraser could be relied upon to give instant and useful oral reviews of poems read by any authors who came along: literary evenings "kept going and held together by . . . his wife Paddy with admirable efficiency and patience." It is good also to read what he has to say about Edwin Muir and his poems, "the best, I thought, that were being produced by a British poet [1950]. . . . Yet he could write without irony about 'being introduced to the Third Programme' by a man [Hamburger] almost forty years his junior."

The memoirs are enriched by several portrait-sketches on quite a large scale, very well written, those on Herbert Read and Peter Höfler, two very different men, are especially good. Among his relatives, we see his father, an eminent and conscientious doctor: "a difficult case would worry and upset him to a degree hardly conceivable now that medicine tends to be practised rather like a motor mechanic's skill," and his mother, patient, understanding and unselfish, doing her best for the family in all sorts of difficult circumstances.

Reading what I have written, I feel that Michael Hamburger may appear to have been presented as a "poet's poet" and this will never do. So he is, certainly, but he is a reader's poet first. And his beautifully written prose in *A Mug's Game*, whilst fascinating to poets and critics, will be chiefly enjoyed as a moving, informative and highly entertaining account of those thirty years in the life of an interesting man.

—*Lines Review* 49, 1974

THE LIFE STORY AND REAL ADVENTURES OF THE POOR MAN OF TOGGENBURG
By Ulrich Bräker, translated by Derek Bowman (Edinburgh University Press).

On rare occasions we come across a book for the first time, and wonder why it is not one of these few books that everybody knows as an old friend. In the case of this autobiography, written in

German by a Swiss, Derek Bowman's is the first translation in English: we may wonder why no such translation had appeared for nearly two hundred years, and how it is that this volume, published four years ago, is not already very well known. But we may be thankful that Mr Bowman has made such a good job of it, racy, sympathetic, appropriately colloquial, easy of movement and backed by all the scholarship we would require. Just to give the flavour of the thing, here is a sample of Ulrich Bräker's account of himself as a soldier in the army of Frederick the Great of Prussia, in a war that was none of his business, having been sold to a recruiting-officer by a confidence-trickster, an acquaintance of his father's:

> You won't be expecting from me a detailed description of our camp between Königstein and Pirna as well as of the Saxon one facing us at Lilienstein. . . . I write only about what I've seen, what went on immediately around me and particularly affected me. As regards the most important things, ordinary blighters like us were most ignorant, and not really bothered either. The only thing that interested me and so many others like me was—how to get to hell out of it and back home!

It does ring true, this Other Ranks' view of active service; the style of the translation is just about right for our time, as any squaddy will agree, and works for us as that of the original must have done in colloquial German of the eighteenth century.

But the style can rise to an occasion, as in the goat-herding episode, which places Bräker's book along with the nature-literature of that period of developing Romanticism. Here is a passage describing the life of a real herd-boy:

> If, however, I did win the field and gained sunlight and the bright sky above me, with that great sea of mist under my feet and here and there a mountain jutting up like an island—why, what joy, the glory and the gladness of it! Then I wouldn't leave the mountains for the whole day, and my eye could never see its fill of the sun's rays playing on this ocean, and waves of vapour in the strangest shapes swaying about over it, until towards evening they threatened to rise over me again . . . lonely birds flapped around overhead, dull and sullen, and great autumn flies buzzed so dismally about my ears that I couldn't help weeping. Then I'd

freeze even worse than early on and feel pains in my feet, even though they were as hard as shoe-leather.

Bräker is writing his life-story for the edification of his children, in the hope that they may follow his intentions of living a pious and useful life, and learn from his shortcomings which have so often caused him to fail. So he is able to describe his terrible hardships without asking us to feel sorry for him; rather he is asking God to make allowances for his weakness, and hoping to show his children an example of honest endeavour in the hope that they may do better. This is one thing that gives his story that quality that might be expected to make everyone love it, especially as it is told with his unique kind of rueful humour.

A delightful example of this humour is the way he talks about his wife, whom he refers to as "Dulcinea." She appears to have been very good for him, though not in every respect agreeable:

> While I was going round burning my saltpetre I saw a girl pass by one day with the face of an Amazon which quite impressed me as an old Prussian . . . I made discreet inquiries after her; and I rather liked what I gathered; except for one main point, she was said to be really rough—as regards temper, not morals!

He admired his wife, though he "never felt that tender inclination towards her, generally named love" and his account shows that she stood by him throughout his struggles to keep his family together, and was a really excellent wife, except for her noisy determination to have her own way, especially as she often knew best anyway. All this is presented with literary skill, and yet the reader is led to believe what he says, that he is a bungler in everything he tries, which adds to the charm of his book, as we accept the convention of its artless author.

We may accept this the more easily because of the complexity of Bräker's character. He was, first, a Pietist writing his autobiography as a religious duty: Mr Bowman's Introduction is informative about this kind of writing. But he belonged also to the Romantic movement, and partly shared, for instance, Goethe's attitude to writing as an art. Here again, the Introduction is very useful, pointing out that "the great writers, like Rousseau and Goethe, drive a new idea or feeling to its limits where a lesser writer still lingers half in older conceptions." Bräker, to whom moral goodness came first, was not writing under so powerful an artistic impulse.

Bräker's honesty, however, frequently has much to do with the reader's enjoyment. His account of a battle, for instance, puts him right in the front line of authors who are not altogether filled with military ideas of virtue:

> Then all my courage sank into my breeches; my only wish was to creep into the bowels of the earth, and a similar fear, indeed deathly pallor, could soon be seen on all faces, even of those who'd always made out how tough they were. Emptied brandy flasks (every soldier has one) were flying through the air amidst the general rain of bullets; . . . in front of me, all was fire, smoke and fumes; behind me many more troops coming on, rushing towards the enemy, to the right two main armies in full battle-array. Finally to the left I saw vineyards . . . just the odd Prussian, pandour or hussar dotted about. . . . There! that direction, I thought; otherwise you haven't a hope in hell!

War does not, in fact, take up much of this book, which is more concerned with trying to lead a good life, mostly in circumstances that make it nearly impossible to earn a living. Love, also, enters largely into his story, but to a less extent than marriage, which is not the same thing. There is an idyllic account of Bräker's love of his first sweetheart, Annie (though "could she talk!—a proper magpie she was") and of the quiet ending to that affair, which Mr Bowman in the Introduction contrasts with the story of Werther. Bräker's 150-odd pages are crammed with vivid incident, character-drawing and description, the quantity of which is not easily indicated in words except in the form of a list; though the liveliness, I hope, may be appreciated from these few samples. For instance, there is an extended, detailed and brilliant description of the recruiting-officer temporarily on duty just beyond the control of his superior officers. Many comrades, including one real bad egg, Bachmann, cross his path, appear, vanish and sometimes turn up again; each is swiftly brought to life on the page.

This first-hand account of a poor man's business affairs will also provide exact historical sources that in a more "literary" and less factual work might be less reliable or altogether lacking. While just a boy, besides looking after his father's goats, Bräker tried to earn his keep by selling sticks. Nobody would buy his hard-won faggots, but at least he tried. And how interesting and unfamiliar his occupations are to us!—saltpetre-burning and gunpowder-making, and dealing in, spinning and weaving cotton yarn, which he bought at two florins the pound, during a fairly successful period; "my profit that year, however, didn't amount to more than 12 florins," he says. "But even that seemed a princely sum to me at the time."

Mr Bowman's 46-page Introduction with its descriptive bibliography, cannot be too strongly commended, I think. Though it moves lightly, a student could gain a very useful knowledge of the history, politics, economics, philosophy, literature, and culture generally of the Enlightenment, by using his references as a reading-list and his remarks to elucidate the whole. It may be asking too much, but I wish he had included the tune of the Swiss song, "Ranz des Vaches." But he does supply its out-of-the-way reference to an entry that I was delighted to find in my *Nouveau Dictionnaire Illustré* by P. Larousse (1899): "*Air que les bouviers suisses jouent sur la cornemuse*." Like a song we wot of in the British Army, the soldiers were liable to be put on a charge for singing it, because (in Mr Bowman's translation of Larousse) it "drove some soldiers to desertion, others to suicide and plunged all into a profound melancholy."

—*Lines Review* 50, 1974

R. S. Thomas and Andrew Young
SELECTED POEMS 1946-1968
By R. S. Thomas (Hart-Davis, MacGibbon).
COMPLETE POEMS
By Andrew Young (Secker & Warburg).

R. S. Thomas writes these poems as an onlooker "of the bald Welsh Hills." He looks at people, rather than at animals or plants, so without fear of pathetic fallacy he may attach his own feelings to the objects of his observation; but in "A Peasant," from *Song at the Year's Turning*, 1955, the opening poem of his collection, he straightway produces an unusual effect that gives the tone of the volume as a whole. Having introduced Iago Prytherch as "Just an ordinary man" (of these parts), telling how he passes his days and nights, he says, "There is something frightening in the vacancy of his mind," and goes on to describe the "stark naturalness" of his clothes, and how he "preserves his stock, . . . Enduring like a tree under the curious stars." So Iago Prytherch, for all his human name, is to be respected as one of a well-adapted natural species. The most curious thing about him, apparently, is that he doesn't seem to mind being as he is: so we might fallaciously wonder about some bat or beetle. Thirty-odd pages later he is allowed to speak for himself, in "Invasion on the Farm," from the same volume:

> I am alone, exposed
> In my own fields with no place to run
> From your sharp eyes.

He complains that this exposure to the poet's observation has laid him open to "the cold winds of the world." But the poem is only putting R. S. Thomas's words into his mouth while he goes on docking mangels; we know quite well that, as we saw him ploughing in the earlier poem, it did not occur to him that he was

> churning the crude earth
> To a stiff sea of clods that glint in the wind—

though that is evidently a clear and realistic statement of what the poet saw. R. S. Thomas, very well-read, with a trained mind and developed aesthetic sensibility, is not pretending to speak as a peasant; no scrap of dishonesty is to be found in this collection; but he shares his surroundings and must make poems out of his world, as in "Soil," from the same volume, where the peasant does not even have a name:

> This is his world, the hedge defines
> The mind's limits; only the sky
> Is boundless, and he never looks up;

even the word Peasant, title of the first poem in this collection, is evidently chosen with care and honesty: not many poets these days would commit themselves to a position in which that word might thus be used.

This poem, "Soil," may be regarded as of a pair with "Welsh Landscape," which it follows with a sense of recovery after despair: ". . . aware / Above the noisy tractor . . . You cannot live in the present, / At least not in Wales . . . There is only the past, / Brittle with relics, . . .

> And an impotent people,
> Sick with inbreeding,
> Worrying the carcase of an old song."

But a powerful metaphor links the opening of "Welsh Landscape" to the end of "Soil."

> To live in Wales is to be conscious
> At dusk of the spilled blood
> That went to the making of the wild sky,

—and so the first poem of the two develops a line of thinking and feeling that leads to despair. But the second poem takes a new turning. He (Iago?) is cutting swedes

> And if sometimes the knife errs,
> Burying itself in his shocked flesh,
> Then out of the wound the blood seeps home
> To the warm soil from which it came.

(Notice, in passing, his practice of firming-up his line with two strong syllables at its end.)

The natural surroundings of these poems are stony, wet and grudging; you wonder how people come to be here at all, struggling to grow something to live on, out of this marginal land. Animals and plants are well adapted, or they would not be here, but people have to manage somehow, whether or no. They may be none the better for the presence of R. S. Thomas observing them so keenly; so he leads us to believe, but these poor circumstances are where he also finds himself, and that is a problem his resolutely honest poems must take as part of their subject matter.

Much later in the collection, in "There" from *Pietà*, he is still looking on, "like a meddler from the town" at "those that life happens to," full of wonder that they can

> give thanks
> In a chapel whose stones are wrenched
> From the moorland.

And still he refuses to console himself and us with some sort of answer.

The last poem in this collection is not about Wales, or even about people; it offers relief, not an answer, watching the martins, those

201

well-adapted birds. But there may be a hard answer, implied throughout the book, that people are more marvellous even than these birds, in adapting their minds and souls to conditions their bodies can hardly endure.

The language and metres of these poems make no concessions either: all the quotations given above will illustrate the effectiveness of his vocabulary (*exposed, spilled, shocked* . . .), plain words rendered unusual by their precise placing (the knife errs, burying itself; shocked flesh; spilled blood (no cliché for once); stiff sea of clods . . .), and clear statements (*passim*). Earlier poems in this collection often achieve a buffeting effect by withholding expected rhymes or supplying unanticipated rhymes or assurances (*e.g.* "Song"); others have a polished cruelty about them, the result apparently of matching consonants but not vowels (*e.g.* "Pisces"). There is a vigour about his verse that seems to come from its near-regularity, and the placing of strong syllables:

> There was Llew Puw, and he was no good.
> Every evening after the ploughing
> With the big tractor he would sit in his chair,
> And stare into the tangled fire garden,
> Opening his slow lips like a snail.

And here also we have an example of marvellous imagery, used sparingly, that takes us by surprise in this excellent poetry, only a few of whose procedures I have attempted to pry.

The poetry of Andrew Young (1885-1971) also is presented very much as that of an onlooker, but there are fewer people in it, and many more animals and plants. The reader is likely to receive an impression of the poet always out for a walk in the country, on the Quantocks or within sight of Jura, in Teesdale or Kent or Northumberland, at least so far as his nature poems are concerned; and of all his work these are likely to be best known and most warmly loved, at least with some sense of awe. But we are assured by Leonard Clark, who has arranged and introduced these Complete Poems, that this must be considered the definitive edition, so the bulk of it is added to by the dramatic works, "Nicodemus—a Mystery," "The Death of Eli" and the dialogue, "Boaz and Ruth," and by the long eschatological poems, "Into Hades" and "A Traveller in Time." The book is excellent value, and it seems wrong to complain, but the reader may feel that the poems might have been less tightly packed into its 357 pages. If they had been grouped under dates, Andrew Young would have been seen more clearly, spanning more than half a century, writing consistently in his own style, while literature was passing in and out of all the phases described in history books of that period. This body of poems is marvellously refreshing and encouraging to one's faith: poetry quietly asserts itself, and not a single lecturer in English Literature, one confidently believes, can do anything about it. Leonard Clark informs us that Andrew Young would behave obligingly towards those who wished to publish his poems, but showed no inclination to press them upon the public. We are not told whether he showed any interest in criticism, but we may guess that he did not, at least so far as his own poems were concerned. He certainly did not write these poems for reviewers; this is a book to keep within easy reach and to read often, where the pages happen to open; and they will tend to open at the nature poems.

These are the work of a very good botanist: that is the first thing to keep in mind. He knew how Nature works. Why it does so is another question; at least his scientific knowledge is not to be faulted, we may believe. And yet he was aware of Nature's power over him, and that was a mystery, though he knew at least which explanations would *not* serve. Here is a sixteen-line poem, "The Secret Wood," in nearly regular verse that mostly rhymes just as the rhymes happen to fall, it appears, but in places casually does not. The poet is looking at an old tree

> That years ago dry sawdust bled
> But sprouts each spring a leaf or two
> As though it tried not to be dead,

and in particular he looks at a broken bough

> That keeps its withered leaves till now,
> Like a dead man that cannot move
> Or take his own clothes off,

(that line, being unrhymed, by chance, it would appear, comes with an added shock. Any kind of regular verse often is most effective when it seems to break). He wonders, and does not know, what makes him look so intently that he fears that someone may disturb him, and concludes,

> I only know
> Though all men of earth's beauty speak
> Beauty here I do not seek
> More than I sought it on my mother's cheek.

His country walks, then, are no simple pleasure trips. Reading more and more of those many short poems, we come to share something of his fascination and his actual fear. He is a very powerful poet indeed, and the power of his poetry is coming out of something common to human nature, primitive or atavistic or whatever. The controlled unfailing suavity of his style, formed no doubt in Edinburgh before the turn of the century, when he received, and played truant from (so we are told by Mr Clark) the best accepted education, serves him now in good stead to make his meaning clear and powerful: rhetoric used as it was intended, ruthlessly and without violence. It is easy to appreciate how the publication of these poems may have seemed to Andrew Young somewhat agreeable but of no great importance to one who would "start with sudden fear" at the sound of the cuckoo. And he knew exactly what he feared: it was the passing of spring, the swift passage of time taking life along with it. And always there is in these poems the awareness that animals and birds do not know this fear, though they are so much afraid of occasional dangers; there also lies part of Nature's fascination. In a late season, he notes, a bird will build its nest in a nearly bare tree if it must, and does not suffer from anxiety, so far as we can see. Nature works by ruthlessness that in human terms can be terrifying: the spider, "Villain of her Greek theatre" (his imagery can be very startling as well as apt) is viewed with a very grim sense of humour:

> From twig to twig a speckled spider,
> Legged like a hermit-crab, had tied to her
> Invisible web with WELCOME
> For sign, and HOME SWEET HOME.

Many of these poems, indeed, are simple and enjoyable, which makes the collection all the more convincing, and so much the more powerful in its total effect, because it is never morbid.

Andrew Young's poems stand up well in the company of R. S. Thomas's, beside whose impersonal and unsparingly penetrating work a great deal of more agreeable poetry looks rather trivial. This is the result of a pressure set up by the interaction of what R. S. Thomas sees and what he believes, expressing itself in such a variety of ways that we are impressed by his fertility of unusual thoughts, even in this not very large book. A few quotations out of context may convey some feeling of this pressure: "The tall Cross, / Sombre, untenanted, / Aches for the Body . . ."; ". . . a bird . . . / Hammering its notes home / One by one into our brief flesh."; "There are other people / In the world, sitting at table / Contented, though the broken body / And the shed blood are not on the menu." The pressure increases throughout this Selection, which is in chronological order ending (too early: one wonders why) at 1968.

R. S. Thomas is a clergyman in the Church of England, described on the jacket, somewhat vaguely, as a priest, but his parish is very different from Canterbury, where the influence of the Comforter is perhaps more strongly felt than in Wales: there, "The Reverend Elias Morgan, B.A." is never far away, in his hill chapel:

> But for some there is no dawn, only the light
> Of the Cross burning up the long aisle
> Of night; and for some there is not even that.

Andrew Young, however, a Scot whose native language was always at command to enrich his vocabulary, became a Church of England clergyman in England, and in his later days "greatly enjoyed the visits he paid to Chichester Cathedral for his annual sermon." His religious pieces are more Biblical than those of R. S. Thomas, and less immediately urgent, though excellently written and admirable, as, for instance, is his hymn, "Lord, by whose breath all souls and seeds are living," which is everything a good hymn ought to be. And yet the Anglican assurances do not seem to cover the procedures of Nature that are associated with our own; and we find in the greater part of his poems a pressure such as that exerted by R. S. Thomas's plainer, but no less accomplished poetic style: the art of both, it appears, comes of a struggle with self.

AT THE HEICH KIRK-YAIRD
By Alastair Mackie (Akros Publications).

This heich kirk-yaird is in Ardnamurchan, where the drowned crew of a curragh were buried: "They kirsent it Ardtoe— / the heich deid-hole." But the poem's title belongs, it seems, to the Highlands in general, hence the cheerless and powerful conclusion:

> Let it be I say.
> Oor will be done. Let the caravans fyle
> the machair and the fremmit tourist's
> camera click on Hielant gaitherins
> and a thoosan year terminal coma.
> Let it be. There's nae mendin for't.

The sequence gives an account of an autumn motor-run past Ben Dorain and by Glencoe and Moidart to a dreich-seeming holiday place. It is vivid, like a travel article, but too honest to please a holiday-agent, *e.g.* describing the reality of pleasure-motoring: "We're fower stoonds in a metal box." They come to hate their "black bummer" and the bad roads, but neither does he like

> . . . the tarmac's airn-grey carpet,
> that couldna hide for me even nou
> the tashes o skailt bleed
> in the lang-syne loupit snaw.

The poem here is telling of a motor-trip through Glencoe, and simultaneously making a clear, though figurative, statement on a deeper level concerning an earlier time, that gives a twinge of conscience about coming to this place on a pleasure-outing. We are never spared such twinges for long; and nowhere is it any use trying to dismiss the terrible past:

> I ken I ken
> we've supped it aa afore,
> the cauld kale o history.

The poem also functions on a third level, since the holiday is being experienced by a visitor, a kind of foreigner, even, who is familiar from his reading with still more foreign ideas that he must take into account: those of Vosnesensky, Baudelaire, Lenin. . . .

The language of this poem-sequence also contributes to the

situation for being foreign to these Gaelic parts of Scotland, more so even than English, it seems. It is a near-conventional Lowland Scots, not so much of a literary language as Mr Mackie used in *Clytach*, his previous book; and this is in keeping with his present purpose. It moves easily; we must admire his mastery of Scots in this conversational tone, in keeping with the narrator's presence here as a tourist, observing curiosities abroad:

> Hou lang will it lest?
> "Ah" he said, "it should be clearing by mid-day.
> About three o'clock."

> It was anither clock he worked till,
> aulder nor oors. It knappit on here
> in this westrin fauld, to the thunder
> and sough o the Atlantic.

This quotation also shows one of several neat devices that link the sequence together. Elsewhere we read of approaching autumn: "Inside us we maun hae a clock that tells / the cheenge o season to oor haill body, . . " Similarly, the "skailt bleed" of our second quotation above, is echoed thus, four pages later: "O bonny the haemorrhage i the settin sun!" This follows the lines: "the land is left alane aince mair / to get on wi its death," and this has its echo after four more pages:

> It got on wi its ain death.
> The sun biled awa its spittings
> and whit was left
> the sea took back intill its muckle mou.
> It was never missed.

This ends a small calamity to set against the huge one of the Highlands, the death of a stranded jellyfish tortured by children: "That shotten ee for aa their howkin / kept gaupin back." And that reminds us in turn of a woman mentioned in another connection on the previous page: "She was the lane ee o the tenement. . . ." So this sequence of poems is pleasing as a composition and has an agreeable tone, though the substance of its argument is uncomfortable and gloomy: Gaelic civilisation is dying in the midst of its beautiful scenery, and that is spoilt by cars and caravans, and somehow insulted by "the English voices in the caravans"—"Whit road do they get my dander up?" he asks. "This is nae Poland, nor are they Nazis."

The reader may be left with doubts about the whole thing. Perhaps it would not be so very different in the Highlands today if the Red Soldiers had never arrived, except that there might not be so historical a reason for resenting the accents of Lancashire and Surrey. The caravans do look conspicuous, but that might be remedied by a draconian measure requiring them to be camouflaged in heather-mixture. As for "the tarmac's airn-grey carpet," you might think the better of it if you had seen these roads before they were made, as the old rhyme has it. Perhaps it is just as well that "It's aa cheenged Duncan Ban," now that it looks as if the mountains may provide a decent living for deer-farmers. And so on. . . .

However, if Mr Mackie's poem-sequence may leave us with thoughts of this kind, that goes to show that it is working on one more level in addition to the three we have already mentioned.

—*Lines Review* 51, 1974

Biographical Notes

J. K. ANNAND (b. 1908) worked as a schoolteacher in Edinburgh. Since 1973 he has edited the magazine of the Scots Language Society, *Lallans*, and as well as editing *Early Lyrics by Hugh MacDiarmid* (1968) and *A Scots Handsel* (1980) he has published *Two Voices* (1968), *Poems and Translations* (1975) and *Songs from Carmina Burana* (1978). His collections of bairn-rhymes have been popular: *Sing it Aince for Pleisure* (1965), *Twice for Joy* (1973) and *Thrice to Show Ye* (1979). His latest publication is *Dod and Davie* (1986), a translation into Scots of Wilhelm Busch's universally popular *Max und Moritz*.

D. M. BLACK (b. 1941) works in London as a Jungian analyst. His collections of poetry include *With Decorum* (1967), *The Educators* (1969), *The Old Hag* (1972), and two volumes in the Lines Review Editions series, *The Happy Crow* (1974) and *Gravitations* (1979).

DEREK BOWMAN (b. 1931) grew up in Liverpool; he has taught Modern Languages in Germany and Britain and is at present on the German Department of Edinburgh University. His publications include a translation of Ulrich Bräker's *Poor Man of Toggenburg*; his poems have appeared in various magazines and in a collection called *Out of my System* (1976).

J(AMES) B(OWMAN) CAIRD (b. 1913) worked for Her Majesty's Inspectorate of Schools (Highland Division). He has taken an active interest in Scottish literature, giving lectures (mainly at French universities) and writing articles. He is married to the poet and novelist Janet Caird.

ALISTAIR ELLIOT (b. 1932, Liverpool) has translated Verlaine (1979), Heine (1979) and Sophocles (1986); his poetry includes the collections *Contentions* (1977), *Talking Back* (1982) and *On the Appian Way* (1984).

IAN FLETCHER (b. 1920) was educated at Dulwich College and Goldsmith College, saw war service in the Middle East, and has taught at the universities of Reading and Arizona. He has written both verse and criticism.

ROBIN FULTON (b. 1937) edited *Lines Review* from 1967 to 1976 and the associated Lines Review Editions. His books include *Contemporary Scottish Poetry* (1974), *Selected Poems 1963-1978* (1980) and *Fields of Focus* (1982). He edited Garioch's *Complete Poetical Works* (1983). He has lived in Norway since 1973 and has translated several Swedish writers.

HAMISH HENDERSON (b. 1919) has since 1951 worked for The School of Scottish Studies in Edinburgh University, where he has been particularly active in the collecting of traditions, songs and stories from Scotland's oral culture He edited *Antonio Gramsci: Letters from Prison* (1974) and his collection of war-time poems, *Elegies for the Dead in Cyrenaica*, first published in 1948, was republished in 1977.

JOYCE HERBERT has published both short stories and poems in a variety of magazines. Poetry Wales Press brought out a collection of poems (*Approaching Snow*) in 1983.

MAURICE LINDSAY (b. 1918) has since 1967 been Director of The Scottish Civic Trust. He has been very active as a magazine-editor and anthologist and has written several topographical books. His critical works include *Robert Burns: the Man, his Work, the Legend* (1954, revised 1971), *The Burns Encyclopedia* (1959, revised 1970 and 1980), and a *History of Scottish Literature* (1977). His *Collected Poems* appeared in 1979.

ALASTAIR MACKIE (b. 1925) taught in Orkney and then, since 1959, in Fife. His poetry has been notable for the skill with which he has handled a rich Scots vocabulary—e.g. *Soundings* (1966), *Clytach* (1972) and *At the Heich Kirk-Yaird* (1974).

SORLEY MACLEAN (b. 1911) is widely regarded as the leading Gaelic poet of his generation. He spent much of his life as a schoolteacher, mainly in Edinburgh and then in Plockton. His first publication was with Robert Garioch, in *17 Poems for 6d* (1940), and then his famous *Dàin do Eimhir agus Dàin Eile* appeared in 1943. He was represented along with others in *Four Points of a Saltire* (1970) and *Nuabhàrdachd Ghaidhlig* (1976), and then a *Selected Poems—Reothairt is Contraigh (Spring Tide and Neap Tide)*, *Taghadh de Dhàin 1932-1972*—came out in 1977.

EDWIN MORGAN (b. 1920) taught at Glasgow University from 1947 to 1980, being titular Professor of English for the last five years of that period. As a poet he has been prolific in many genres and he has also been very active as a translator and essayist. The main gatherings of his work are: *Essays* (1974), *Rites of Passage: Selected Translations* (1976) and *Poems of Thirty Years* (1982).

MICHAEL SCHMIDT is a publisher (Carcanet Press), editor (*PN Review*), critic and poet.

T. C. SMOUT (Christopher Smout) was Chairman of *Scottish International* at the time of the correspondence included in this book, and had just completed *A History of the Scottish People, 1560-1830*. He subsequently became Professor of Economic History at Edinburgh University and, in 1980, Professor of Scottish History at St Andrews.

ANTONIA STOTT was born and educated in Milan and spent much of her working life teaching in Scotland, mainly in the Italian Departments of Glasgow and then Edinburgh University. She produced plays for the Scottish-Italian Circle in Edinburgh, the Italian Department of Edinburgh University and an amateur company. She is now retired and lives in Kent.

BOB TAIT (b. 1943) was full-time editor of *Scottish International Review* (1967-73). Robert Garioch and Edwin Morgan were his co-editors throughout. Along with Isobel Murray, Bob Tait wrote *Ten Modern Scottish Novels* (1984). He is a lecturer in Education at Aberdeen College of Education.

SYDNEY TREMAYNE (b. 1912) worked as a journalist in England between 1929 and 1974, after which he returned to Scotland to live in Wester Ross. His *Selected and New Poems* (1973) gathered work from six collections published between 1946 and 1969.